Think Outside the Inbox:
The B2B Marketing Automation Guide

David Cummings
Adam Blitzer

Leigh Walker Books

Published by arrangement with
Leigh Walker Books
Atlanta, Georgia

10   9   8   7   6   5   4   3   2   1

ISBN 978-0-615-36181-9

To our parents

*With acknowledgments to the others who helped
make this book possible:*

*Laura Folio, Jennifer Betowt, Chris Heiden,
and the rest of the Pardot team*

Contents

Chapter 1. Marketing: What's New?

If you're in our demographic—that 40% of the nation's population that is under 35—you may never have heard of the Fuller Brush Company. But during the 1940s and 1950s, the company's fabled sales representative, the ubiquitous Fuller Brush Man,* became a cultural icon, inspiring comedy routines, several movies, and at least one song. Dressed in a suit and tie and carrying a suitcase of samples in his hand, he embodied the American business ideals of personal service and quality products as he went about knocking on doors, introducing himself to strangers, making his polite but informative pitch, and generally excelling in that coldest of all cold calls.

While nothing might seem less relevant in a book on

---

* The Fuller Brush Company, founded by Alfred C. Fuller in 1906, still employs independent distributors (Fuller Brush men and women) for direct customer-facing sales. Not surprisingly, however, all of their consumer and commercial products can now be purchased online.

marketing automation than conjuring up the image of this quaint door-to-door salesman from bygone times, he serves as a useful reminder of everything that has *not* changed, fundamentally, in the sales cycle. In fact, the typical Fuller Brush salesman, planning out his sales day on an ordinary Monday morning in 1954, actually faced some of the same challenges as online marketers do in today's global market.

In 1954, our Fuller Brush Man (FBM) needed to identify his potential customers. He needed to get out there and put his message in front of those prospects. He had to provide the information and assistance that his customers required to become sales-ready, and finally he had to close the sale. Once our FBM had his customer's signature on the dotted line, however, his job wasn't over. If he was smart (and didn't want to be a one-sale wonder), he'd be sure to follow up with his customers, continually staying in touch so that they wouldn't forget about him or his products. He would certainly devote some time and attention to those leads that weren't quite ready to buy.

The sales cycle today is fundamentally the same as it ever was. There really *isn't* anything new for marketers to learn with regard to the basic phases and progression of making a sale. And the relatively simple marketing methods employed by our FBM in 1954 actually *do* still work today. (If you doubt it, just recall the last time you opened your front door to that adorable neighborhood child selling gift wrap or cookies.) Yet with the advent of the internet and the rise of web marketing, some things are radically different. New complexities have emerged in today's sales cycle, and online marketing presents more obstacles—and more opportunities—than ever before.

The bigger block

To begin with, the marketing landscape and the traditional sales territory both look quite different today than they did two generations ago. Unlike the FBM, today's online marketers don't have a circumscribed neighborhood, a geographic boundary, or a dedicated physical territory in which they can operate unchallenged. The internet has rendered those old geographic constraints irrelevant, and the new territory represents an increasingly bigger "block." For the most part, this lack of physical limitations works to a marketer's advantage, but it also demands far more resourceful and imaginative ways of seeking out and courting prospects.

And it's not just that there's far more competition in the bigger and bigger block. Modern-day consumers navigating the web's boundless frontier have so many more choices now as to where they can begin their buying process. These changes in landscape have had a direct influence on sales reps' effectiveness. In the days when salespeople acted as gatekeepers of company information, providing that information gave them direct access to, and multiple opportunities to build relationships with, their prospects. Nowadays, prospects usually gather their own information independently, so the traditional influence of salespeople has declined significantly.

The faceless customer

The sheer anonymity of internet marketing brings with it enormous challenges. It's not just that we don't know where our customers "live" in the vast digital wilderness— we don't know what they look like, either, nor do we have many clues as to their personalities and individual needs. In fact, the modern customer is so far removed from us that, despite cultivating customer relationships for many months or even years, we may well never meet that customer in person. In turn, we're also faceless to our customers, which only complicates the inherent challenges of forming relationships and of building trust. We need to work much harder, not just to stand out from the crowd, but simply to become "real" in our customers' minds.

It might seem ironic, but it's no coincidence that as more and more buying processes go online and the internet makes transactions increasingly impersonal, social media channels are proliferating. Marketing gurus are starting to speak about web commerce entering an era of social marketing and relationship marketing. The fact is that, however much we sense that we're often dealing with faceless corporate automatons (or their software), most of us would vastly prefer to buy from real people. The rise of social media is in a large sense a reaction to the crushing depersonalization and anonymity of the new marketplace.

The longer sales cycle

Let's face it: It just takes longer to complete the sales cycle than it used to, particularly for business-to-business (B2B) marketers. The term *B2B* refers to companies who sell products or services to other companies or enterprises. By some analysts' estimations, the average B2B sales cycle is already 22% longer than it was just five years ago.[1] In this extended and highly fluid buying process where decision-makers are added to and subtracted from the buying mix through a seemingly revolving door, sales reps can invest considerable time and resources pursuing deals that never materialize. Prospects have more choices now and need more time to evaluate them, so salespeople who have fully invested themselves in an extended sales cycle risk being reduced to mere unpaid consultants when the deal goes south.

In terms of completing his sales cycle, the FBM of yesteryear could often move a prospect through the entire buying process in one productive stop. But today's B2B marketers have got to be in it for the long haul, because the modern sales cycle is a lengthy process that requires constant attention. This shift has created a paradox in that contemporary sales and marketing teams must focus significant energies on creating ongoing and sustainable relationships with prospects while simultaneously seeking ways to shorten the sales cycle.

The more complex sales cycle

Today's sales cycle has become increasingly complex for the B2B marketer. Buying decisions now involve many people with multiple perspectives, many of which may be cross-cultural. Decisions frequently involve complicated situations and multi-faceted problems, the solutions to which can often be difficult for the customer to understand. In addition, these decisions often require large financial investments; in today's tough economic environment, even what were formerly modest expenditures must now be heavily scrutinized and justified.

Adding complexity to complexity is the bidirectional nature of today's sales process. The FBM of the 1950s had only a few ways to reach out to Jane or John Doe. His prospects had only one way to acquire information about his company and products, because he was the gatekeeper of that information. His usual method of contact was ringing doorbells, but he could also employ direct mail or place a personal telephone call to make sure he stayed top of mind with his prospects. But the internet—first through email, and then with the explosion of corporate websites and e-commerce—opened up a flood of opportunities for marketers to reach out to their prospects, and made it easier than ever for prospects to reach back. More recently, undercurrents have appeared in that great digital flood, in the form of a whole new variety of different channels and touchpoints for bidirectional customer contact.

Brian J. Carroll has written extensively about the complexities in today's sales cycle. In his book, *Lead Generation for the Complex Sales Cycle,* he points out that "astute marketers today recognize that there is an entire sphere of influence represented by contacts associated with the economic buyers, e.g., influencers, information gatherers, opinion molders, and an external sphere of end users." All of them, Carroll says, "must be addressed with equal intensity. The more you reach the better."[2]

This is good advice, of course. But Carroll's injunction places an additional expectation on already overburdened marketers. Now we must market to everyone, all at once, all the time. And we must to do it in a way that counters the anonymity of the digital sales territory. Finally, we must work to put a face on ourselves and get to know our faceless customers before we can start building sustainable relationships for the long haul.

How can today's B2B marketer possibly manage all of this? What is the most effective way to confront the challenges of a sales cycle that, while unchanged in its fundamental human dynamics, has become longer, more complex, and more impersonal? How can marketers best address—"with equal intensity," in Carroll's words—the entire sphere of influence around our prospects?

THE RISE OF RELATIONSHIP MARKETING

Much of the answer, as more and more businesses are discovering, lies in technology itself. From the earliest beginnings of the internet revolution, software and systems have been designed and called upon to manage the customer relationship with the goal of shortening the sales cycle and increasing revenues. The earliest efforts to do this came in the form of database marketing in the 1980s. Originally amounting to little more than automated contact management, database marketing mainly consisted of a company's customer service staff interacting with that company's clients and taking notes. Although it represented a vast improvement over the FBM's manual spreadsheet and hand-printed Rolodex, the early implementation of database marketing wasn't exactly a seamless process, and the compiled information on the existing databases tended to be disorganized and hard to track, update, and retrieve.

In the 1990s, companies began to improve on database marketing by initiating more of a two-way conversation. Instead of simply gathering data for their own use, companies began giving something back to their customers in the form of gifts or incentives for their continued business. This was the beginning of customer retention programs—the loyalty programs that we've become familiar with through airline frequent flyer programs, bonus points on credit cards, and the gifts and coupons we're routinely offered based on tracking of our customer activity and spending patterns. Technology was employed as a way to passively increase sales while actively improving customer service. It was out of this environment that the concept of Customer Relationship Management (CRM) was born.

Although more and more businesses began adopting CRM systems as the decade progressed, the promising field of customer relationship management encountered some significant stumbling blocks. Implementations were often fragmented and incongruous, with individual departments working on isolated initiatives that addressed only their own needs. Siloed thinking and decision-making frequently produced separate and incompatible systems, conflicting prospect information, duplicated efforts, and dysfunctional processes that reflected a fundamental misalignment of goals. Typical deployments of CRM systems were so lengthy and expensive that small and medium businesses were simply left out in the cold.

It has only been in the last few years that two additional evolutions have occurred, helping bring true customer relationship management within the reach of small and mid-sized businesses and enabling these businesses to address the lack of technical integration and human collaboration that marked earlier CRM adoptions. The first of these is cloud computing, which allows common business applications to be accessed through a web browser by storing applications and data on remote servers. Smaller companies can now get many reliable enterprise-level services without incurring the capital expenditure of traditional CRM. The result has been a kind of leveling of the playing field, wherein smaller newcomers can begin to compete with more established players.

The second evolution in customer relationship management has been the development of marketing automation and lead generation systems. The success of these technologies, which build bridges between intra-company departments by harnessing and sharing data and metrics through an intuitive, user-friendly interface, has given rise to the concept known as **collaborative customer relationship management**, whereby sales, services, finance, and other departments can readily see the impact of marketing decisions on the rest of the company and on prospects and customers. The effective use of these tools for lead generation, customer communications, and tracking and reporting functions has minimized the traditional rift between sales and marketing. Multiple tailored and personalized multi-touch campaigns now replace the mass campaigns of yesterday, with the positive byproducts of increased customer satisfaction and loyalty.

This book will focus on best practices for marketing automation, the latest stage in the evolution of relationship marketing, and it is aimed at B2B marketers who target small and mid-sized businesses. According to Forrester Research, annual spending on customer relationship management is expected to top $10 billion this year,[3] a clear indication of how much faith companies have placed in the ability of CRM tools to help grow revenue, improve the customer experience, and boost productivity of customer-facing staff. This figure represents enterprise spending; smaller companies have historically been priced out of the market, leaving them unable to take advantage of the efficiencies that CRM affords to marketing and sales departments in larger companies.

But marketing automation is proving to be a game-changer. Marketing automation solutions can be deployed quickly and affordably, and packages can easily be tailored to suit different company needs. Most importantly, marketing automation tools enable non-enterprise businesses to address many of the obstacles that are unique to today's longer, more complex, and far more impersonal sales cycle. They can help to combat the "faceless customer" phenomenon by creating multichannel, highly targeted, and personalized campaigns that ultimately lead to real-time, one-to-one customer relationships. They can bridge the gap between sales and marketing by delivering more qualified leads and by simplifying the lead assignment process. They can enable businesses to capitalize on their current investment in customer databases, existing websites, and other marketing collateral, allowing companies to wring every bit of useful data from these existing assets so that they can continuously improve marketing strategies. Finally, marketing automation solutions can return actionable metrics and reporting to determine campaign effectiveness and return on investment (ROI).

While marketing automation promises all this and more, it is still a relatively new phenomenon. Its uses are sometimes poorly understood, and there is often confusion about the capabilities that distinguish marketing automation from other tools that automate certain marketing processes. In addition to these problems, the vendor landscape for marketing automation can be confusing in and of itself.

The goal of this book is to outline the functions of a marketing automation platform and to describe its range of capabilities and benefits. It will also provide best practices and advice gleaned from companies that are already taking advantage of the full potential of marketing automation. If your B2B company is considering adopting a marketing automation solution to enable collaborative customer relationship management, the information here will also help you ask the right questions and distinguish between various vendor claims in order to find the right balance for your company on the price-performance continuum.

Chapter 2. A Clearing in the Cloud

The growth of the internet dictates a shift in marketing emphasis—and stretched marketing budgets—away from traditional channels in favor of online vehicles. Change has happened so quickly that many companies need help managing their online marketing activities. Your company may be one of these—reasonably certain that you need a solution to automate some of your sales and marketing tasks, but not so sure about what kind of solution you need, or how much it might end up costing. Assuming you're a small or mid-sized business that doesn't expect to have it all (at least not today), how do you know which tasks to focus on now, and which ones to defer?

There is scarcely any online process today that hasn't been automated in some way, but the claims made by many of the newer tools that manage these formerly manual processes can often be confusing. The gaps, or overlaps, in their various functionalities can be problematic, and the terms and acronyms used to describe them can be positively bewildering.

It follows that a good starting place might be with some basic definitions. The subsequent section will define and describe the basic functions and processes of marketing automation platforms, and it will also clarify the alphabet soup of acronyms and initialisms, as well as the technical terms used to describe them. Each definition will also explain how each of these tools relates to, duplicates, or complements the functions of a marketing automation solution.

SALES AND MARKETING SYSTEMS

Customer Relationship Management (CRM) is an evolving philosophy or approach to sales and support, as well as the database solution used to execute and manage that approach. For the purposes of this book, CRM refers to customer database management. The information in a CRM describes relationships in detail so that management, salespeople, and support staff can access information, match customer needs with product plans and offerings, remind customers of service requirements, and learn what other products a customer has purchased, and so on.

Traditionally, the big players in the CRM market have been the on-premises solutions provided by enterprise vendors like Oracle, SAP, and PeopleSoft. However, with the rise of cloud computing, cloud-based CRMs deployed via the Software-as-a-Service (SaaS) model have gained widespread adoption. SaaS-based CRM adoption has been driven by on-demand vendors like salesforce.com, NetSuite, and SugarCRM. According to analyst firm Gartner, the SaaS submarket is growing at more than double the rate of the CRM market as a whole.[4]

> **A marketing automation solution** is a database of your prospects, much like a CRM, but with additional capabilities and features. Marketing automation solutions typically offer an entire suite of marketing tools to help manage these prospects and to automate certain activities. Examples of these features include large-scale email marketing, drip nurturing programs, lead scoring and grading, micro-level activity tracking of both anonymous and identified visitors, ROI reporting, database deduplication, file hosting, and form and landing page builders. While some CRM systems offer a basic subset of similar features, these don't really approach the sophistication of the robust tools contained in marketing automation platforms.
>
> Through bi-directional syncing, CRM and

marketing automation platforms work together to keep all data updated, and a single sign-on simplifies collaboration for the sales and marketing teams. Using the platforms together in a complementary manner allows the strong points of each one to shine, ultimately making life easier for marketers.

While a CRM system may be necessary to support a large sales force, the typical CRM system simply does not have much marketing functionality. Most companies need CRM *and* marketing automation to enable successful collaboration between sales and marketing teams. Since most marketing automation platforms can be easily connected to cloud-based CRM systems, the combined benefits of using both are now within reach even for smaller companies. However, a marketing automation solution can act as a stand-alone tool that can be used independently to manage a prospect database even without a CRM. Small and mid-sized companies without the budget for both will get better value by first adopting a marketing automation platform.

Content Management Systems (CMS) are used to store, organize, and facilitate collaborative content. CMS solutions run the gamut from Enterprise Content Management (ECM) platforms, enterprise-wide platforms that manage all of a large organization's unstructured data, to highly specialized systems that manage content for particular industries. Content management systems are further subdivided by the types of content they manage. There are CMS solutions that manage only web or mobile content, for example, on a small or large scale.

➢ **A marketing automation solution** functions as a mini-CMS for marketing content in several ways. Marketing automation platforms are able to create, organize, and publish content and images for marketing campaigns and websites through reusable content blocks. The content is created in user-friendly templates and can be tailored to individuals by inserting data elements (*"Dear [First_Name]"*), as well as by executing rules that select different messages based on the situation. For example, a rule might send different messages or offers based on the customer's account balance, or it could display a personalized call-out on a website based on the profile associated with a visiting prospect.

Even though most campaigns are channel-specific, many elements of them, such as logos and text blocks, are shared between different channels. Managing these reusable components through a single platform makes it easy to deploy changes, while ensuring consistency and reducing the amount of work that goes into creating multiple targeted and tailored campaigns.

Campaign Management Systems (also abbreviated **CMS**) are used to design campaigns, to schedule and execute them across multiple channels (including print, phone, email, and the web), and to track their effectiveness. Different types of specialized systems exist for direct postal mail campaigns, for automated phone calls (robocalls), and for storing and delivering marketing content and advertisements to mobile phones and PDAs. The **Email Service Provider (ESP)** is one example of a campaign management tool for email only.

➢ **Marketing automation solutions** are legitimate campaign management systems in their own right, capable of creating and managing ongoing marketing campaigns and components, in addition to managing the underlying marketing database. Integrated into marketing automation platforms are user-friendly solutions for landing page building, forms management and file hosting, along with a powerful application for creating and automatically scheduling one-to-one or mass email deployments. Marketing automation can replace an email marketing vendor entirely, particularly for B2B business needs.

Marketing Performance Management (MPM) is a term used by marketing professionals to describe the analysis and improvement of the efficiency and effectiveness of marketing strategies and campaigns. Until recently, the problem with MPM systems was that they were geared toward large companies and were typically so complicated that small to mid-size companies couldn't take advantage of the business intelligence that MPM systems provided. Because most companies were using marketing programs comprised of disparate tools, it was too difficult to extract and consolidate information without significant technical resources. The email marketing tool didn't talk to the CRM, which didn't talk to the lead scoring mechanism, which didn't talk to the web analytics tools. This lack of integration made MPM too difficult for most businesses to implement.

➢ **Marketing automation solutions** provide many of the benefits of an enterprise-wide MPM through analytics and reporting features that are centralized and easy to use. Typically they focus on the results of email campaigns and website effectiveness, providing metrics such as cost per vetted prospect, cost per opportunity, cost per sale, and ROI. Analyzing these metrics helps companies shape their marketing strategy and improve their bottom line.

Sales Force Automation (SFA) systems are generally considered a part of a company's CRM strategy in the marketing philosophy sense, and also of CRM systems in the database sense. An SFA system helps manage all the stages in a sales process. At its core is a contact management system that tracks all contacts made with a given prospect, the purpose of the contact, and any follow-up that might be required. This ensures that sales efforts are not duplicated, reducing the risk of annoying prospects with unnecessary contact. SFA systems also include a sales lead tracking system, which lists and records data on potential customers. SFA solutions are now also available through cloud-based SaaS models on a subscription basis.

➢ **Marketing automation solutions** share an over-lapping contact management database with SFA systems, but they also provide the marketing interface that complements the sales interface of SFA systems. Whereas SFA systems are used by sales personnel for manual calendaring and logging of sales calls and contacts made, marketing automation platforms *automatically* record prospect activities and use the resultant information to grade, score, and nurture leads. They then feed this marketing data into the SFA system so that the sales rep can act on it. In some companies, the marketing automation platform acts only as the front end for leads, handing them off to the SFA system once they are deemed sales-ready. For other companies, the marketing automation platform continues sending out emails and tracking activities based on prospect interactions—information that can be collected and used later to nurture prospects until they are ready to buy. Ideally, SFA and marketing automation should continue to work in tandem even after the sales rep has engaged with the lead.

Web analytics tools are able to capture data from multiple channels and sources, store it in a common data model, and use modeling to perform analytics and segmentation tasks. Google Analytics is an example of a free web analytics tool. Omniture, Webtrends, and Coremetrics are some examples of paid subscription providers. These analytics tools supply macro trends related to web traffic: number of hits, number of unique visitors, geographic information, most popular pages and keywords, the average amount of time that visitors spend on a page, and so on. This kind of information can be priceless for companies looking to maintain a competitive edge.

➤ **Marketing automation solutions** provide a view that complements the one afforded by web analytics tools. Macro-focused tools like Google Analytics look at the big picture, while marketing automation tools are micro-focused, collecting information on individuals. Where the macro-focused tool might tell you that the majority of your website visitors are located in the northeastern United States, the micro-focused tool will reveal that a specific visitor—John Doe, the vice-president of a specific Massachusetts technology firm—has come to your site seeking information.

Marketing automation solutions don't replace existing web analytics tools, but they do piggyback off them by incorporating data for micro-analytic reporting. While no marketing strategy can afford to ignore the big picture, the real goal is always to learn about that individual who might become your customer.

Bid Management Software is used for management and reporting of paid search marketing across search engines. This software automates the bidding in pay per click (PPC) auctions driven by web search engines like Google and Yahoo!.

➤ **Marketing automation solutions** offer invaluable reporting capabilities for companies using paid search as part of their marketing strategy. A marketing automation platform can be connected to application programming interfaces (APIs) like those supplied by

Google AdWords to automate daily downloads of cost data and number of clicks generated by an ad campaign. The marketing automation platform then pairs this data with prospects generated from that spend, and also with sales that were closed in the CRM, in order to show exactly how much revenue was generated for every dollar spent in Google AdWords on a particular search term. This data enables companies to close the loop around money spent on advertising and money generated in revenue.

Customer service software, also referred to as customer support software, is aimed at capturing, managing, and responding to customer contacts. However, this software doesn't inherently provide any comprehensive, real-time analysis of those interactions for use in multichannel marketing campaigns. It is typically used to manage help desk tickets or call center contacts.

➢ **Marketing Automation solutions** can add value to customer service software, particularly for technology companies who offer free trials as part of their sales process. Marketing automation tracking code can be added to the knowledge base, FAQ pages, or the trouble ticket system within customer service software in order to provide insight into customer needs and behavior. As prospects who have downloaded the software explore the knowledge base, read articles, post inquiries in forums, or submit help desk support requests as part of their software evaluation process, these activities are continually logged. This aggregation of behaviors determines the prospect's score, serving an important lead qualification function for the sales rep. The tracking ability of a marketing automation solution can also improve the quality of customer service by revealing a customer's questions and frustrations (based on how often they return to a particular topic) and enabling companies to proactively reach out to them with helpful advice or additional assistance.

SIMPLICITY. ECONOMY. CONTROL.

B2B companies have been trying to tailor B2C-focused tools to their needs for years. Email marketing, web analytics, and paid search tools have long been staples in a marketer's arsenal, but the data captured has always been aggregated and siloed. Marketing automation makes it possible to control these formerly disparate marketing and sales channels from one central interface and to gain tremendous efficiencies and intelligence throughout a complex sales cycle.

The beauty of marketing automation is that it puts small

and mid-sized businesses in the marketing driver's seat. Marketing automation is simple to deploy, operate, and maintain, allowing marketers to achieve total campaign management through the consolidated power of as many as ten discrete tools, all without the help of IT. Marketing automation offers the quickest path to the simplicity, economy, and control that marketers crave.

What Do You Call It Again?

Marketers haven't yet agreed upon what the emerging field of marketing automation should be called. Comprehensive suites of marketing automation tools first emerged over a decade ago, although the concept of automation itself was nothing new at the time. The earliest vendors of these platforms called them **demand generation** solutions. While this term is still used from time to time by marketing experts such as David Raab, it has fallen out of favor as a name because of the term's use by large enterprises dealing with supply chain management.

Marketing research firm Forrester Research has long used the term **lead management automation (LMA)** in its surveys and reports on the growing field, as have blogs like LeadSloth. Research and advisory firm Sirius Decisions regularly releases reports on what it terms **demand creation.**

Marketing automation has emerged in the last few years as the preferred terminology for this kind of platform. Marketing research authorities MarketingSherpa and Gartner have both adopted this phrase, along with most vendors in the field.

Chapter 3. The Four T's of Effective Email Campaigns

With the tools and systems that are used to automate marketing processes now defined, it will be easier to grasp how marketing automation actually replaces these tools, or complements them, when marketing automation technology is used for what it was ultimately developed to do: save you time and improve your bottom line.

Most marketing strategies these days are based on email marketing, so it helps to understand the basic elements of a successful email campaign. Some of the following tips and tricks have been hard won by others who are using email marketing to its fullest potential. Consider this collection of advice as a set of best practices for email campaigns.

The elements of a great email marketing campaign are based on what we like to think of as the **Four T's**. To get the optimum results from your campaign, you need to **tailor** it, **test** it, **time** it, and **track** it.

TAILORING

The foundation of any good email campaign always lies in the design itself—those carefully chosen words and pictures that make up an email advertisement or invitation. Spending sufficient time laying the groundwork here will pay off later in the form of greater response rates, better branding, and stronger customer relationships. Clearly you shouldn't take shortcuts in improving your creative, but marketing automation has made the process considerably less tedious and time-intensive while also enabling the customization, or tailoring, of email campaigns for more personal, customer-friendly messages.

CREATING CONTENT

Marketing automation platforms with a "what you see is what you get" (WYSIWYG) editor make it easy to design and author professional-looking HTML emails. A WYSIWYG editor provides a user-friendly editing interface that closely resembles that of familiar word processing applications and approximates how the page will actually be displayed in a web browser. The familiar interface eliminates the need to learn HTML and allows for fast editing of content that can be tailored to your desired messaging. The interface also facilitates the easy insertion of images like headers or logos, as well as custom HTML code for further tailoring to your brand. Aside from the WYSIWYG editor's capabilities, you will still have the ability to achieve advanced formatting using HTML, as well as the option of using pre-designed templates to get the look you want.

Here are a few simple Do's and Don'ts for content creation:

✓ **Do make sure your message is readable and simple to act on.** Get your message across in as few words as possible; make sure you choose those words carefully. Naturally, all of your content should be sufficiently clear and straightforward to be understood without any further explanation. But no line demands more clarity and readability than your subject line.

✗ **Don't underestimate the power of a good subject line.** The vast majority of email inboxes today are crowded and cluttered with competing demands for the reader's time and attention. Your subject line can make the difference between getting your content read and having your message trashed instantly. Subject lines should be relevant to the recipient and should correspond to or sum up the content of the email. Don't underestimate the sophistication of your recipients. A subject line with catchy or clever wording could elicit a smile or generate a little goodwill, which ultimately means getting your email opened and read. But tread carefully: Corny, cutesy, or misleading subject lines will most likely backfire and alienate prospects.

Research shows that while shorter subjects optimize open rates, longer subject lines tend to optimize click-through and click-to-open rates. Subject lines that contain key pieces of information make it easier for recipients to decide if an email is relevant to them. Also keep in mind that the more words there are in a subject line, the greater the likelihood that the email will appeal to the right people, and you will have reached your target audience.

✓ **Do make your content relevant.** It's simple: Your message must be important to its intended audience. Some of the burden of ensuring relevant content falls on the task of building the email list itself. An outdated list that includes inappropriate recipients will almost certainly ensure that your content won't be meaningful for many of those who receive it. There are ways to get cleaner, better data; these will be discussed later. The main takeaway here is that having a murky message or irrelevant content will prevent you from reaching your target audience.

✗ **Don't overload your recipients with too much information or too many offers.** People are already suffering from information overload as it is. Don't let your email further overwhelm your prospects with superfluous information or multiple calls to action. Keep it simple and focus on getting your main message across concisely.

✓ **Do make unsubscribing easy.** The damage to your reputation that can result from a missing or buried unsubscribe link just isn't worth it. Make sure you include a clear way to opt out or unsubscribe in the email template.

WRITING PERSUASIVE CONTENT

The copy writing and copy editing phase of your campaign message is critical to how it will be perceived by its recipients. *What* you say is important. But so is *the way you say it*. To get the best results, your emails must distinguish themselves from the typical generic sales pitch. Blatant sales emails get ignored; informational, conversational messages get results. The winning formula is a combination of tone and substance. To make your email campaigns more persuasive, you should:

✓ **Cut the hype.** Avoid the meaningless superlatives and sales buzzwords. Savvy consumers can see right through overblown hype, and more often than not, they will interpret it as a smokescreen for an insubstantial product. Think of those TV infomercials with the outrageous claims and over-the-top testimonials. The featured items come off more like bogus potions peddled by a snake oil salesman than quality products sold by a credible company. That's obviously not the impression you want to leave with your prospects.

✓ **Know your audience.** You should really know your audience, from their needs and wants to the kind of language they use. What are their problems? How can you offer solutions? Blanket emails targeted at generic problems are a turn-off because they suggest that you haven't taken the time to really get to know your prospects and their needs. Every prospect wants to feel as if you understand them and their problems and have their best interests at heart. You need to convincingly express the value of your product in terms that apply specifically to that individual and to his or her problems and needs.

✓ **Keep it simple and get to the point.** You certainly don't want to patronize your recipients or dumb down your message. But prospects don't want long-winded messages that seem to harbor an ulterior motive. They want a simple, straightforward message without any marketing mumbo-jumbo. They don't open your email thinking, *"Wow, I wonder what the special offer could* be?" What they're *actually* thinking is, "*OK, what's the catch?*" It's important to get right to the point and say what you mean. Also remember that many email preview screens reveal only about ninety words, so make sure you can express your main idea concisely in the first few lines of your email.

✓ **Strike the right tone.** Use the same conversational tone you'd use with a respected friend or colleague, making sure to balance formality with familiarity. Ideally, you want to create the impression that you are a trusted friend sharing valuable information with your prospect—not an obnoxious interruption trying to make quota.

✓ **Back it up.** The cardinal rule of persuasive writing is being able to back up your argument with evidence. It follows that a successful marketer should be able to provide concrete examples or hard data to support the claims they make. Ultimately, you want your emails to be persuasive enough to get a conversion, and the best way to persuade prospects is to give them the proof they're looking for.

Marketing trainer and coach Karen Talavera suggests that getting a good response rate to any email campaign often depends on engaging the customer in a dialogue.

Ideally, your communication should resemble a two-way exchange rather than a one-way announcement. Talavera offers these additional tips for getting that dialogue going:

✓ **Adopt a conversational tone, not a promotional one.** Approach the message as if you are writing a friend to share something important with them. Avoid sounding like you just want to sell them something.

✓ **Use your brand to add personality to your message.** Talavera mentions some current examples, such as the GEICO gecko's endearing spiel or William Shatner's goofy Priceline antics. Elements of your brand should come across in your message, whether through tone, style, or even graphics.

✓ **Get customers involved.** Customers love getting interactive, and one of the easiest ways to do this is to invite them to give feedback on your site or product. You can invite them to submit reviews, testimonials, or success stories. This essentially amounts to free promotion and is a win-win situation for both customers and marketers. User-Generated Content (UGC) has long been the key to success for web companies like Amazon.com. It gets your customers involved by making their experience interactive, all while adding significant value to your own website.[5]

Many people genuinely enjoy taking quizzes or completing surveys. Encouraging this kind of interactivity is a great way to get a dialogue going. Engaging your leads in a dialogue will not only drive sales, but it will create more informed and interested customers who are more likely to buy from a trusted source.

PERSONALIZING CONTENT

If the *least* effective email marketing campaign is the generic blast—a widespread electronic blanketing of your customer database with an impersonal, undifferentiated message—then it follows that the *most* effective campaign would entail thoughtfully sending a personalized one-to-one message to each of your prospects. Unfortunately, it may not always be possible (or economically feasible) to achieve this kind of one-to-one messaging. But marketing automation tools make it easier than ever to customize your content to make emails more upfront and personal.

Dynamic Content

Dynamic content, or conditional content, is messaging that can be changed based on preconditions you determine. The dynamic content made possible via marketing automation allows you to further tailor customized prospect messages. This functionality can be set up to perform a variety of customized actions, such as displaying unique content to different demographics or market verticals. And because marketing automation platforms employ user-friendly templates, they make it easy to achieve several basic types of customization.

Variable Substitution

The message templates offered by marketing automation platforms contain fields which represent values or recipient attributes that can be tailored to fit specific marketing goals. These fields, also called *dynamic tags*, can be used for personal greetings, reference to specific purchases or customer interactions, and similar variables. The use of variable substitution goes back to the birth of word processing software and its groundbreaking adoption by the direct mail industry. While we might now be habituated to receiving "personalized" mail of all kinds, this was pretty exciting for the early recipients of campaign material from the Publishers Clearing House Sweepstakes who got to see their own name on a million-dollar check.

These days it's not so much the *To* variable of an email message that gets our attention. More often than not, it's the *From* line that matters. The ability to tailor reply addresses can greatly improve the probability that an email will be opened by its recipient. People are accustomed to receiving marketing communications from generic email addresses like *info@yourcompany.com*, but B2B marketing is all about building a relationship—something that's hard to do with a generic sender address. A form email from a generic address is not nearly as effective as one sent directly from the sales rep who has already been working with the customer. Unfortunately, most B2C-focused email tools force you to adopt one *From* address. To really personalize your message, make sure your email system can send from the recipient's assigned sales rep. This small touch will impress many recipients, and it also allows any replies to be sent directly to the appropriate individual.

Content Insertions

Larger blocks of content can also be developed as dynamic or conditional content, but a word of warning is in order here. Because dynamic content is kept separate from the message template, the task of editing it is also separate from that of your larger creative. Content must be created, proofread, and approved out of context, a process that requires extra care and diligence.

SEGMENTING LISTS

One of the easiest tailoring operations you can perform on your database—but also one of the most powerful—is list segmentation. Segmentation divides your database into unique groups, enabling you to deliver a different group-specific message to each segment. Segmenting allows you to match content to recipients' interests, thereby forming a connection in a way that can't be achieved through a generic email blast.

There are many options for segmenting these key groups based on your specific product. Targeted email campaigns can be easily created and distributed by using marketing automation tools to generate segmented lists. There are a number of ways you can segment your email lists. These are outlined below.

Geographic Segmentation

This is one of the most obvious ways of dividing up prospect lists for targeted campaigns. Adding a little local flavor to your emails can help give prospects the feeling that you know and understand their interests, even from halfway around the world. For example, one promotional products company was able to increase its open, click-through, and buy rates 20-50% simply by crafting targeted emails that contained product samples featuring local sports teams that correlated with each respective geographic segment. Geographic segmentation is one of the most straightforward and effective ways to connect with your prospects.

Behavioral Segmentation

Behavioral segmentation divides your prospects into groups

depending on their behavioral profile. For example, you could classify frequent visitors to your website as belonging to one segment, while another group might be comprised of prospects that have downloaded white papers. You can then send targeted communications to groups of prospects based on their interests; the first group (frequent visitors) could get an invitation to sign up for a webinar, whereas the other group (white paper readers) could get an email with a link to download another related white paper.

Setting up a group of automation rules that sends messages based on user activities and behaviors is known as drip marketing. Drip programs help you to easily create a multi-touch campaign to reach new and returning visitors. For example, you can set up rules to automatically send out an introduction email to a prospect who has requested information, followed by a pricing list three days after their last visit to your site, and a special offer one month later if they still haven't responded to your call to action. Drip marketing and automation rules will be covered in greater detail in *Chapter 5 - Staying in Touch.*

Purchasing Power Segmentation

Segmenting according to purchasing power is one more way you can create targeted email campaigns. Collecting data on your prospects allows you to create campaigns that specifically target key leads. This kind of data can be especially helpful if you sell multiple products to different industry verticals. For example, a particular software solution might be appropriate for IT departments, but another one might be more helpful to HR departments. A targeted campaign would ensure that the HR manager receives only relevant information on the latter product, rather than a generic catalog of all your offerings. You can also use this technique to ensure that your email goes to CEOs or other decision-makers instead of less targeted prospects.

Segmenting is nothing new for B2B marketers, but it is no longer the tedious manual process it once was. Marketing automation makes list segmentation not only worth doing, but easy to pull off as well. Using segmentation as a tailoring technique can significantly boost opt-in and click-through rates while allowing you to create more personal messaging that speaks to your prospects' interests and needs.

LOOK AND FEEL

The first decision you'll need to make in determining how your campaign email will appear to recipients involves deciding whether your email formatting will be in HTML or plain text. This decision is made within the email template itself, and most marketing automation solutions also allow for a multipart (text plus HTML) option.

Plain Text vs. HTML

Senders today almost always prefer HTML for its flexibility and visual appeal, but you should weigh the advantages and disadvantages of each format before ruling out plain text altogether. These are laid out below.

Plain Text offers:

- **Universal readability.** While HTML is undoubtedly more visually appealing, it lacks the universal readability of plain text. Every email client can render plain text emails, so using it means that you never have to worry about your formatting being a stumbling block to deliverability. Also, the rise in popularity of mobile email clients (cell phones and PDAs) means that some people actually prefer plain text over HTML because the text-only format displays cleanly and easily on mobile devices.
- **Higher deliverability rates.** Plain text messages generally achieve a slightly higher deliverability rate. Since spam filters can't read images, HTML emails are more likely to be classified as spam. Another issue related to deliverability is file size. Plain text emails are smaller and require less bandwidth to deliver than HTML emails, so they're more likely to be delivered successfully.

- **Consistently accurate rendering.** Most government agencies and large corporations in certain industry verticals routinely strip out HTML elements from incoming emails to protect against viruses, causing such emails to display improperly. If you want your email to render exactly as you intended, plain text is best.

HTML offers:

- **Better click-through rates.** The click-through rates of HTML are close to twice that of plain text emails. This can be largely attributed to the visual appeal of HTML over plain text. It is more inviting to click on a button or an image than it is to simply follow a basic embedded link with no visual cues. If you want to ensure better click-through rates, HTML is vastly preferable to plain text.

- **Tracking codes.** HTML offers the ability to place tracking codes in links to help you determine the effectiveness of email offers. Such codes can make the link look long and scam-like in a plain text newsletter, for example. Also, while plain text emails don't allow you to track open rates, HTML makes this possible.

- **Enhanced aesthetics.** Your message's attractiveness and readability can be appreciably improved with color, graphics, and font choices. However, having these options can make HTML formatting more expensive.

The plain text vs. HTML decision is one that email marketers continually struggle with, and for good reason. Marketers want the impact that HTML offers, but they also want their message delivered, understood, and appreciated. There are three important "big picture" points that should be taken into account when assessing the alternatives. You should consider that:

- **HTML is not a universally interpreted language.** An unfortunate consequence of using HTML is that different programs can render HTML differently. For example, the creative that looks flawless in Microsoft Outlook 2007 may be misaligned and hard to read in Outlook 2003.

- **Email clients don't always load images by default.** The client might not support HTML, or recipients could have images turned off. Perhaps of more relevance to B2B marketers today is the growing popularity of mobile devices. It's increasingly likely that recipients will be reading your messages on an iPhone, a Blackberry, or some other mobile device, and images and other HTML features won't render correctly in these platforms.

- **Content is king.** The final point to remember when assessing the plain text vs. HTML debate is that content rules. Don't let the tail wag the dog when designing your creative. Images should add to, not detract from, your message. An email cluttered with too many images and objects is frustrating due to its implied demand on the reader's time and attention. An HTML email that's nothing but one big pretty image might not reach its recipient at all if a spam filter misinterprets it as a trick and trashes it. And graphics that render only as a bunch of red *X*s in the preview pane most definitely won't support or enhance your copy.

In the end, it all really comes down to knowing your audience. B2C firms that market directly to consumers tend to go with visually appealing HTML emails. If your target audience is in an industry with strict email regulations, such as government entities and public agencies, you might want to consider going the text-only route. Most B2B marketing automation platforms allow you to send out both options at once (*multipart formatting*) so that recipients will receive emails in the format most appropriate to their preferences or their email client's requirements.

Color and Design

While the color and design elements of an email marketing campaign need to be consistent with your branding, you don't need to go so far as to make every piece of a single campaign part of a perfectly matched set. The marketing creative for your email marketing should be consistent with that of your website and landing pages, but sometimes it's even more effective to have a creative that varies slightly from medium to medium. Maintaining a harmonious creative provides a consistency of experience for your brand, but introducing slight distinctions might stimulate more curiosity.

Regardless of the decisions you make in terms of images, it's crucial not to miss the opportunities that your top-line message presents. Since your message may be viewed in a preview pane with images turned off, or on an email client or PDA that doesn't support HTML content, your top-line message should include a link to a web-based version—just in case. You can also use informative alternative text for when images are turned off.

TESTING

Once you have the creative that satisfies your marketing goals, and once you've made the decisions that will best tailor it to your customer base, you'll want to monitor your campaign's look and feel by testing it in several different email providers. It's important to see how your email will look, not only in different readers like Yahoo!, Gmail, and Outlook, but also in mobile environments like Blackberry and Windows Mobile.

CAMPAIGN PREVIEW

Although some marketers have numerous email accounts set up for testing purposes, the easiest way to view any email in the 50+ email clients available today is through a campaign preview feature like the one in Return Path or LitmusApp. A campaign preview feature can identify content and delivery issues and test against spam filters, ensuring that your email renders exactly as you intended.

Make sure to test just one variable at a time. Identify content issues like spelling and grammar errors that will affect your reputation. Also take note of your message's appearance. Do your images display correctly? What does your creative look like in the preview pane or with images turned off? You should also test all links in the email to confirm that they work properly. To ensure optimum deliverability, send the test email to multiple addresses, including ones with business and free email providers.

OUTSMARTING THE SPAM FILTER

A campaign preview feature is also invaluable for determining if your marketing creative will trigger leading spam filters (like those offered by Postini and Ironport). This testing technique will also help you detect whether the problems are with links, poorly formatted HTML, or a high concentration of "spammy" words and phrases.

Spam filters are always changing, so it can sometimes be difficult for marketers to get legitimate messages delivered to prospects and clients. If you find that your test emails are getting sent to the "Junk" folder, follow these steps to remedy the issue:

✓ **Test a text-only version of your message.** This will help you diagnose if the issue is content-related or code-related. If the text version gets through to your inbox but the multipart version does not, the issue may be with your images or the source code for the HTML. Make sure you're not using external Cascading Style Sheets (CSS) links. All styling should be inline.

✓ **Avoid spammy words.** If you have determined that the issue is with your content, remember that certain words and phrases can be interpreted by spam filters as spammy, especially those related to money, discounts, or free offers. Try changing a few keywords (or even omit them completely for testing purposes) until you pinpoint the problem. You may need to strip out content sentence by sentence to find the issue. It's also a good idea to study the Readme file for Microsoft Office Junk E-Mail Filter, as well as any similar documentation for spam filters within other email clients.

✓ **Check your image-to-text ratio.** Too many images or images that are too large in comparison to the amount of text in an HTML email can be considered spammy. Adding more text or reducing the number and size of images may help. Also, make sure that your images include alt attributes that contain the alternate text that should be displayed when the images don't load.

✓ **Check your text styling.** Excessive use of all-caps text, too many different font colors (especially red, green or blue), or smaller- or larger-than-average font sizes (10-12 point fonts are standard) can all be interpreted by filters as spammy.

✓ **Make sure your content does not include styling from Microsoft Word.** If you are pasting in content from MS Word, use the "Paste from Word" button in the WYSIWYG editor to avoid having extra styling tags pulled in, which can make the HTML spammy.

✓ **Check for SenderID and DomainKeys records.** As a final precaution, verify that you've added SenderID and DomainKeys records to your Domain Name System (DNS).

All of these steps will improve the deliverability of your emails, but the single most important step you can take to outsmart spam filters and get your messages delivered is to set up email authentication, which is covered in the following section

THE BENEFITS OF EMAIL AUTHENTICATION

Even ethical marketers find it difficult to get past automated spam and phishing filters that can't differentiate a legitimate email from a dangerous message. One way to dramatically improve your deliverability and prevent cases of mistaken identity by overzealous spam filters is to set up email authentication. This step is sometimes ignored by marketers because it is not absolutely required to send emails and can often require the assistance of the IT department. But because such measures are a reflection of a company's integrity, the price for ignoring authentication is really too high for legitimate marketers to bear.

Authentication Standards

Email authentication involves equipping automated emails with enough authentic, or verifiable, information so that recipient mail servers can recognize the nature of each incoming message automatically. This differs from content filtering, whereby an email is blocked or allowed based on an analysis of its content rather than its source. Authentication standards attempt to separate the unethical "black hats"—spammers and phishers—from "white hat" marketers who operate legitimately.

Currently, there is no universal set of authentication guidelines, but there are some widely-adopted standards used by a growing number of ISPs, webmail services, and other mail servers. The four most commonly accepted standards are SPF, SenderID, DomainKeys, and DKIM.

- **Sender Policy Framework (SPF)** authentication allows network administrators to specify which internet hosts can send email claiming to originate from that domain by adding a specific SPF record to the public DNS record. Mail exchangers can then verify the sender's identity against the list published by the email administrator.

- **SenderID** authentication validates the origin of email messages by verifying the IP address of the sender against the alleged owner of the sending domain. Sender ID is the email authentication tool supported by Microsoft, while DomainKeys (below) is Yahoo!'s tool.

- **DomainKeys** is a Pretty Good Privacy (PGP) protocol for authenticating email that employs a public and private key. Senders publish a public key for their domain, and all outgoing email is cryptographically signed using the corresponding private key. The advantage of DomainKeys is that it protects both the integrity of the sender *and* the message, instead of just checking to see if the IP address is allowed to send the message, as is the case with SPF and SenderID. This method not only verifies the validity of the sender, but it also allows third parties to relay or forward the message without breaking the authentication.

- **DomainKeys Identified Mail (DKIM)** is Yahoo!'s and Cisco's combined attempt to enhance the DomainKeys standard. This protocol bases acceptance of messages on the sender's overall reputation and trustworthiness. DKIM uses the cryptographic validation technique of DomainKeys to evaluate whether to accept email from the sender's domain.

The major ISPs and many corporate spam filters check for one or more of these types of authentication when deciding whether or not to allow emails into a recipient's inbox. A marketing automation solution that allows you to send emails from your actual domain (rather than the dummy domain typically used by email service providers) and automatically authenticates using these four commonly accepted standards will go a long way in reinforcing your company's legitimacy and safeguarding its reputation, ultimately ensuring that more of your emails get delivered.

TIMING

Sometimes it seems as if you've done everything right. You're pleased with your marketing creative, and you've customized it to meet your business goals by being as dynamic, personal, and customer-friendly as possible. You've proofed your content, checked for image display issues, and tested for technical errors. It looks great, and everything works as it should. Yet your campaign is just not making the impact you had hoped for. Could the problem be with bad timing? What *is* the best time to send emails to prospects, anyway?

The unequivocal answer is: *It depends*. If you're a B2C marketer promoting a Caribbean vacation package, the best time for your offer to arrive in a prospect's inbox might be on Friday evening or Saturday morning, when her mind isn't on the office and she can daydream about sunshine and ocean breezes at her leisure. But if you're a B2B marketer, that same timing probably couldn't be worse.

B2B marketers should follow these general rules of thumb about timing in order to increase the chances that their messages get the attention they deserve:

- **Don't send emails over the weekend or on Mondays.** Prospects are already dealing with a stack of weekend email, and you don't want your best efforts to get lost in the shuffle.

- **Avoid sending emails over major holidays or typical vacation times.** Email tends to pile up during these periods, so be sure to time your message so that it doesn't get overlooked.

✖ **Don't send emails first thing in the morning.** You'll be competing with the usual barrage of early-morning email. What makes you think your message will stand out?

✖ **Don't send emails at the end of the day.** They might get brushed aside as your prospects knock off work and go home for the day. Then you're back to square one, and your email must compete with the next day's inevitable early-morning deluge.

✖ **Avoid sending emails when prospects are likely to be away from their computers.** Try to time emails to arrive during the workday while prospects are actually in front of their computers. Lone messages that pop up in cleared-out inboxes during regular working hours tend to get opened and read instantly. This is exactly the kind of placement you want for your message. The times just before lunch or just after lunch are ideal for this strategy.

Think Outside the Inbox

Timing is important not only for email campaigns but also for communicating with prospects through other channels. Many of the timing tips shared here also apply to blog postings, Tweets, or Facebook updates.

Marketing analyst Mark Brownlow has written about the importance of getting the timing right when sending out emails. He offers the following helpful advice on how to analyze the best time to send out emails:

✓ **Analyze send times and response rates from past campaigns.** Try to identify any patterns that emerge, especially with regard to particular send times that seem to have the highest or best response rates. Brownlow suggests going back about six months and graphing your time-of-send against the response rate. You can then alter your send times to maximize response rate.

✓ **Compare opens-per-hour to send times.** If you graph this relationship, the standard curve should be smooth and even. Bumps in your own data's graph might indicate special patterns or anomalies you should pay attention to.

✓ **Try segmenting your lists by time-of-open.** There is no single send-time that will be optimal for *all* of your prospects; there are going to be different ideal send-times for different segments. Segment your list by time-of-open (e.g., *Opened between 10:00 a.m. and 1:00 p.m.* vs. *Opened between 1:00 p.m. and 3:00 p.m.)* and you'll be surprised at how easy it is to determine the best send-time for each grouping.[6]

One final aspect of timing marketers should consider is the frequency of your contact with prospects via email. You should be sending emails frequently enough to stay top of mind with prospects, but not so often as to become an annoyance. Three emails per year is probably not enough; three per day is definitely too many. The nature of your product or service and the campaign tracking data you gather will help you find the sweet spot between too often and not enough. Marketing automation tools help you strike this happy medium by automating campaign actions based on decisions you've made ahead of time regarding timing and other variables. A marketing automation solution offers considerable time and labor savings by allowing you to create emails and schedule them for future deployments, ensuring that your campaign is timed right while requiring minimal investment from you.

TRACKING

When it comes to discussions of tracking, it is important to make a clear distinction between *testing* (what works persuasively and technically) and *tracking* (analyzing the results of, or customer reactions to, a campaign). Testing comes first; tracking happens later. Testing ensures that your email campaign will be deployed correctly. Tracking produces actionable metrics that can be used to judge the efficacy of an entire campaign or any of its elements (such as the timing of particular email offers) and to compare campaigns to each other.

Email tracking helps you learn whether an email ever reached its intended recipient and whether it was opened or not. Most email tracking tools record the date and time that an email was received as well as the date and time it was opened. Tracking tools also note the recipient's IP address and let you see which links (if any) the prospect clicked on after opening the email.

Most marketing automation solutions include built-in tracking features that measure things like open and click-through rates, as well as bounced (not received) messages and opt-outs or unsubscribe messages. Email tracking yields a number of helpful metrics that can be analyzed to measure the success of a marketing campaign or webpage, in addition to helping coordinate sales and marketing actions.

TRACKING METHODS

Web bugs. A web bug is a piece of code that is embedded in an email or webpage to track user behavior. Also called *web beacons* or *pixel tags*, web bugs are invisible to the user because they arrive as small, transparent GIF files. Web bugs can track the IP address of the computer and the type of browser that fetched the web bug, as well as the time it was viewed, the URL of the web bug or the page on which it was located, and a previously set cookie value.

Click-throughs. Click-through rate (CTR) is most commonly calculated by dividing the total number of clicks (*not* the number of individuals who clicked) by the total number of impressions. For example, if an email offer was delivered 100 times (impressions), and its included link was clicked only once, this would result in a 1% CTR.

Bounced messages. A bounced message occurs when you send out an email that gets returned by the recipient's mail server. Bounces can be either synchronous, which reject the email immediately after you try to send it, or asynchronous, wherein you're able to send the email, but you later get a notification that it was not successfully delivered.

Bounces are also categorized based on the reason for the failed delivery. Hard, or permanent, bounces can occur for a number of reasons. Maybe the domain does not exist or the recipient is unknown, or perhaps the receiving mail server is refusing mail due to a network failure or some other technical issue. This is the sort of bounce you'd expect when you have a bad or invalid email address that needs to be scrubbed from your lists.

Soft, or transient, bounces result from a temporary failure to deliver an email. Soft bounces don't necessarily indicate a bad or invalid address—they're more suggestive of some temporary issue that prevented your email from being sent, so in most cases you should try sending the message again later. Full mailboxes can cause soft bounces, as can trying to send a file that's too large.

The bounce management features of marketing automation platforms typically catch both soft and hard bounces. These are sent to the return path address so that you can process them, scrub any faulty addresses from your email list, and display the bounces in reports. Marketing automation solutions make this process easy; for example, some platforms automatically scrub an invalid email from your list after the first hard bounce occurs, or after a certain number of consecutive soft bounces. Bounce management data is usually fairly intuitive and easy to use. You can easily see who has either been tagged as hard bounce or has opted-out of your email communications altogether.

TAILOR IT, TEST IT, TIME IT AND TRACK IT

Marketing automation solutions offer significant value in helping you master each of the **Four T's** that determine the success of an email marketing campaign:

- **Tailoring** your campaigns to appeal to prospects on an individual level is effortless when you use marketing automation tools to personalize your emails with relevant content and messaging.

- **Testing** can be simplified and automated to ensure maximum email deliverability and to protect your reputation as a legitimate company.

- **Timing** your emails for optimum effectiveness is no longer a perplexing trial-and-error process when you follow best practices to get your timing right.

- **Tracking** features within marketing automation platforms provide a wealth of information for performance evaluation and list management that you can leverage for improving your ROI.

Chapter 4. Looking for Love in All the Wrong Places

Finding the right customers can be like looking for love. Where should you look? Who should you pursue? What are the best strategies?

There are plenty of marketers who pursue the "Dive Bar" strategy of lead generation. They'll get phone numbers at any time, from anyone and everyone, and pass on these unqualified leads-on-cocktail-napkins to their sales team in the hopes that one or two might actually become a customer "love connection." But what really happens is that your salesperson goes on a cold-calling binge and ends up hating himself in the morning, leaving you, his Marketing BFF, feeling as though you should have done something differently. Perhaps you should have set him up with nicer, more respectable leads. The kind you might meet at your grandma's church picnic.

Don't stoop to this level. Be intelligent about your

search, and know when to forego those less-than-ideal opportunities. Don't just throw yourself at every lead that walks by. Your company deserves better than a dive bar.

LEAD GENERATION THE MATCH.COM WAY

A better approach would be to follow the proven strategy of the highly successful Match.com dating site. Start your search by devising an ideal customer profile. Who would your "dream-date" customer be? What qualities would they need to have to make your business relationship work for the long haul? What are their needs, and how can you satisfy them? Just as being choosy with your prospective dates can yield huge relationship dividends later on, so can scoring and grading leads help you to separate the wheat from the chaff and pursue those prospects that would make the most ideal customers.

PROFILING YOUR IDEAL CUSTOMER

Marketing automation solutions employ the Match.com strategy by creating customer profiles and assigning scores and grades to identify how closely those profiles match your customized ideal customer profile. But in order to make this approach work for you, your sales and marketing teams will need to achieve both clarity and consensus on the type of customers your company wants to attract. This essential first step requires marketers to collaborate with their salespeople—the ones who are out there on the front lines every day.

The following questions will get you started on developing that ideal customer profile:

- What size of organization would you prefer to deal with? On average, how many employees would it have?

- In which geographic areas would you prefer that these organizations be located?

- In which market sectors or industry verticals would these organizations operate?

- What are the most likely job titles of the individuals who would be making buying decisions?

- What other positions in the organization might be involved in buying decisions?

Encourage your sales staff to think out loud about their most successful sales and best customers. Ask them to consider the following questions:

- Which existing customers were the easiest and quickest to convert?

- What similarities do these customers possess?

- Are there any specific criteria that would make prospects an especially good fit?

As B2B lead generation blogger Brian Carroll has suggested, once your marketing and sales teams have agreed upon an ideal customer profile, don't stop there. Publish and circulate it so that everyone stays focused on your goals. Review and revise your definition to incorporate real-life experiences with prospects.[7]

Having a clearly defined profile of your ideal customer is the absolute starting point for determining which lead generation strategies work best for you and for improving the effectiveness of your marketing initiatives. You may also discover that once you've begun attracting more targeted customers, asking for referrals becomes easier and generates better responses, since you've started by providing a more precise specification of what you're looking for. With your thinking now distilled and concentrated, your marketing strategies will start to take on real definition and direction.

GRADING

Before assigning leads, your lead qualification or marketing operations team should grade them according to how well they fit your ideal customer profile; this will help your sales reps properly prioritize them. Most lead grading systems start with a default profile that you can customize by setting your preferred criteria (location, company size, job title, etc.) for qualifying prospects You can also create any additional profiles that meet your company's needs, and you can use multiple profiles if you want to target several different audiences. For example, you may have different profiles, and perhaps different grading criteria, for your technical prospects as opposed to executive prospects.

Selecting Your Grading Criteria

When evaluating inbound leads to send to the sales team, lead scoring and grading work together to help you determine your ideal prospects. While scoring happens automatically, without any real setup required unless you want to fine tune it with additional personalization, setting up a grading profile is a bit more of an art. Since grading is designed to help you determine how well a prospect fits your organization, you might want to personalize your criteria beyond the defaults provided by your solution. Sales and marketing should collaborate to come up with a set of acceptable criteria that will help them arrive at a unified vision of what constitutes a good lead.

Sales Lead Insights put together a list of potential grading criteria frequently used in the industry to help you build your own grading profile. Here are some of the suggestions:

- Consider both firmographics (items relating to a target company, like industry or company size) and demographics (items relating to a specific person, like job title).

- Consider the prospect's role in the purchasing decision.

- Consider the fit. Does your product meet or exceed their requirements?

- Consider the prospect's available budget.

- Consider the revenue potential of the deal.[8]

Some of these criteria may be immediately obvious, and they're great candidates for automation based on information collected on forms. Other items that are initially unknowns, like budget and timeline, may become more clearly defined once a sales rep has made contact. Though not as applicable to the sales handoff, it is still beneficial to update the grading criteria as you learn more about a prospect. This will help the sales team prioritize follow-up calls, and it allows both teams to start tracking overall trends.

Defining Grades

Grades are based on explicit information about the prospect, whereas scores (discussed below) are based on implicit activities performed. Prospects with grades of A+ or A are considered a great fit, while those with grades of A-, B+, or B are a good fit, and those graded B-, C+, or C constitute just average fits. Some grading systems can be configured to automatically confer a certain grade on a prospect based on specific attributes, such as belonging to the industry vertical in which your company specializes.

The letter grade assigned to a prospect corresponds with how closely that prospect fits the ideal customer profile, as well as how qualified that customer is according to the criteria you've set. It is advantageous to incorporate a methodology for how grading works in your organization, based on your own custom profiles. For example, when prospect information matches certain desired values, you could adjust grades as follows:

> **Industry** – increase/decrease by a partial grade
> **Department** – increase/decrease by a partial grade
> **Job title** – increase/decrease by a partial grade
> **Company size** – increase/decrease by a partial grade
> **Location** – increase/decrease by a partial grade

Again, it is important to develop a process specific to your organization. Grading can be automated through the use of automation rules, which make grade adjustments based on criteria that you specify. For example, if you wanted to target company vice-presidents as potential decision-makers, you could set up a rule that would place any prospects with this job title into a list that receives emails targeted at executive-level decision-makers. The myriad other uses for automation rules will be discussed in subsequent sections.

SCORING

While grading is based on explicit objective information about a prospect, scoring is based on actions taken by the prospect. Lead scoring adds points for every action that a prospect performs on your website or in response to an email or some other call to action. A prospect can earn points towards their total score by browsing the website, clicking on the link in an email, downloading a white paper, signing up for a webinar, or filling out a web form. You can customize the number of points awarded for particular activities, and you can decide which activities accrue points. For example, simply landing on your page may add only a single point to a prospect's score, but a prospect who enters *"pricing"* in an internal site search may get 10 points, since this action is a far better indicator of purchasing intent.

Here's an example of what a default points system for prospect scoring might look like:

> ➢ **Successful completion of a form** = +50 points
> ➢ **Site search query** = +3 points
> ➢ **Tracked link click** = +3 points

- **Hosted file access** = +3 points
- **Visitor session** = +3 points
- **Visitor page view** = +1 point
- **Form/form handler/landing page error** = -5 points
- **CRM opportunity created** = +50 points
- **CRM opportunity lost** = -100 points

Prospect scores can also be modified by automation rules. For example, an automation rule might be set up so that if the prospects have requested a demo or a particular white paper, 50 bonus points will be added to their scores. You could elect to give 50 points for all form submissions but award a "bonus" to a form or landing page submission that shows a more serious intent (such as filling out a form requesting a free trial). Automation rules can handle all of this behind the scenes. Rules can also be used to give negative points in order to downgrade certain prospects, such as a competitor's employee who is visiting your site purely for investigative purposes.

Customize by Page

Some marketing automation solutions allow you to customize scoring by page, enabling you to add or subtract points based on prospect activities on the individual page level. This would not typically be done on every page, but only on important pages, such as a pricing page or another page that conveys a similar degree of intent. Tracking codes can be also used to give negative points (or subtract points) on, for example, a site's "Careers" page, since the visitor is most likely interested in a job as opposed to your product or service.

LEAD ASSIGNMENT

Marketing automation solutions allow you to automatically assign leads to sales reps when they reach a certain grade and score criteria. Automatic assignments can be done based on a variety of different factors including geographic territories, type of organization, and industry vertical. For example, you could set your preferences to automatically assign all prospects with a country value of *Canada*, *United States*, or *Mexico* to your North American sales representative. Some organizations automatically nurture leads until they reach a specific grade and score threshold. At that point, qualified leads are assigned via a round-robin system to the next available sales rep for follow up. This system allows for a timely and equitable distribution of only sales-ready leads. Some marketing automation solutions can be configured to send out regular updates to sales reps to notify them of new prospect activity on their site within a given timeframe, which helps reps prioritize their efforts and better allocate their time.

A *Bad* Idea for Lead Generation

Buying names for a marketing blast is a bad idea. Why? Because the recipients don't know you, are unfamiliar with your services, and will generally respond poorly to this tactic. Buying a list of "victims" normally produces three results:

1. **High bounce rates** due to unscrupulous acquisition of the names and email addresses (unless a double opt-in is utilized, which is a less shady tactic).

2. **High opt-out rates** because the "victims" have no idea who you are.

3. **Feelings of violation on the part of the recipient.** How would you like it if someone purchased your credit card or social security number from some unscrupulous source and started using it without your permission?

CONNECTING THE DOTS

Connectors are add-on tools that enable marketing automation platforms to sync with third-party applications such as a CRM system or Google AdWords. Data can be passed back and forth between the two applications, allowing a user to easily manage many formerly disparate marketing channels and tools from within a single interface. Connectors provide the essential links needed to sync your own prospect data with external information you collect from various sites and applications. Connecting the dots between these scattered bits of valuable data can help you get a more complete picture of your prospects and their tastes and motivations, maximizing the efficiency of your marketing automation activities and thereby enabling you to better address prospects' needs with the appropriate solutions. The following examples illustrate the types of information that can be shared through connectors.

CRM CONNECTORS

Integrating a marketing automation solution with a CRM system continuously syncs data between the two platforms and allows the sales team to view updated information on prospect activity from within the CRM system. The contact database in the CRM can be sorted by the scores and grades assigned by the marketing automation platform, for example. The continuous sync between the two platforms ensures that data is non-redundant and always up-to-date. Integration with familiar systems also means fewer barriers to company-wide adoption and easier day-to-day use. Most marketing automation solutions offer native integrations with CRMs like salesforce.com, NetSuite, SugarCRM, and Microsoft Dynamics, but others can be integrated via a web service API.

OTHER CONNECTORS

Google AdWords is a pay per click (PPC) advertising medium that allows you to create ads based on keywords or phrases related to your business. Marketing automation solutions can hook into your Google AdWords account and track prospects who reach you through this type of paid search. You can tie cost data from AdWords to opportunity data from your CRM to determine your true cost per qualified lead and search engine marketing ROI.

Google Analytics is an enterprise-class web analytics solution that lets you view and analyze your traffic data. A Google Analytics connector is designed to simplify the flow of information between Google Analytics, your marketing automation platform, and your CRM system. Such a connector enables users of Google Analytics Keyword Tags in URLs to pass those tags into a connected marketing automation platform. Once the tags are set up, the fields can be synced with a compatible CRM system, allowing you to use the CRM reporting features to run custom analysis on your tags.

Data can be collected from all five of the Google Analytics tags: *source*, *medium*, *term*, *content*, and *name*. You could also utilize the connector to create a new campaign based on your Google Analytics campaign tag for any new prospects coming in from tagged URLs.

LinkedIn is best known for its networking capabilities, but it is also a great way to generate leads with the most potential. A great advantage of LinkedIn for finding new prospects is that it allows you to see profiles of people with whom you are not directly connected. This feature lets you look at different people within an organization and choose the ones you'd like to reach out to based on their position and fit with your company's offerings. One particularly useful feature on LinkedIn is the "Get introduced through a connection" option, which allows you to ask a mutual connection to introduce you to a prospect. This option greatly improves your chances of making contact with a prospect because the request is not random or anonymous. Marketing automation solutions that connect to LinkedIn enable you to easily augment prospect profiles by checking out their professional credentials and connections.

Jigsaw (owned by salesforce.com) is another prospecting tool used by sales professionals and marketers to get fresh and accurate sales leads and business contact information. It boasts detailed contact information for over 19 million people. Jigsaw can be connected to a marketing automation platform so that its internal information on your prospects can be easily accessed within your marketing automation platform.

Twilio is a web service API that helps you instantly follow up with interested prospects by phone. This type of pay-as-you-go telephony application can be tremendously useful when used in conjunction with certain features of a marketing automation platform. Twilio can be set up so that when a prospect fills out a form on your website, the assigned sales rep will immediately receive a phone call from the computer which reads out the prospect's information. Cold calling might not be easy, but most salespeople love picking up a ringing phone. What's more is that the advantage of being able to follow up when your product or solution is top of mind for a prospect is invaluable for salespeople.

Twitter was originally intended for use by individuals, but companies are increasingly utilizing it as a marketing and promotional channel. Most marketing automation platforms allow you to tie a Twitter username to a prospect so that their most recent tweets can be easily viewed within the platform. Tweets can provide insight into a prospect's thought process and may provide clues as to their needs or specific pain points you could address when you make contact.

Desktop alert applications provide sales and marketing teams with real-time alerts of visitor and prospect activity. Results refresh periodically to indicate whether visitors have taken specific actions on your company's website. Some marketing automation solutions offer these as a standalone add-on application.

Connectors like the ones described here are valuable tools offered by some marketing automation solutions. Once you've run through a quick setup, connectors make prospect information from the connected applications instantly available in the marketing automation platform's interface. Because connectors help you collect additional information to round out prospect profiles, they make your marketing efforts more effective while greatly enhancing communication with prospects.

SOCIAL MEDIA

A recent HubSpot ebook called *Who's Blogging What* begins with this interesting observation:

> In the closing days of 2009 Pepsi decided against hiring Justin Timberlake, Cindy Crawford or even Britney Spears to speak for them during the 2010 Super Bowl. They would instead take the $20 million and use it to speak directly with—and to listen to—their consumers through the web. It was the final and perhaps the most significant signpost marking 2009 as a year when emerging social media technologies mandated new strategies for anyone who deals with the public. No organization seemed unaffected. Pope Benedict XVI launched his Facebook app in May. In June the US State Department asked Twitter to delay scheduled maintenance because of the role it was playing during civil unrest in Iran.[9]

This passage mentions just a few of the big players who

have jumped on the social media bandwagon, but it powerfully illustrates why marketers can no longer afford to ignore social media. At the end of 2008, Facebook had already outstripped email in terms of worldwide reach, and the commercial pages category is now the largest single category, representing 39% of all Facebook pages.[10]

Social media tools are all about relationships, but they are of most value to marketers for their powerful branding capabilities. Just ask JetBlue, a company that reinforces customer loyalty daily by responding to any and every customer Tweet within minutes. At latest count, JetBlue had managed to accumulate over 1.6 million Twitter followers for itself.[11]

Social media tools provide inexpensive, broad-based channels for lead generation and qualification. They draw users to your website and push your content through their own spheres of influence. While social media channels can require a sizeable commitment of time and attention, it's an investment that can really pay off.

Linking Profiles

Make sure you consistently add your company website to all of your profiles on social media sites. Some social networking sites also allow links to RSS feeds of your blog. Adding these links will generate more visits to your blog and your website.

COMMUNITY MARKETING

A specialized type of social marketing called *community marketing* is typically a corporate-sponsored forum where customers and prospects interact to share feedback about product features and performance. Community marketing has opened up new opportunities for companies to improve their brands through sharing best practices and soliciting candid feedback. Community marketing channels are sometimes referred to as *Web 2.0* applications because they depend on user-generated content and allow users to interact with, add to, or change content. This interaction can take the form of idea exchanges, forums and message boards, wikis, blogs, rating systems, videos, opinion polls, and shared reviews, all of which collect customer opinions and drive increased sales through a more viral approach to marketing.

The challenge that lies in community marketing is the policing of inappropriate comments and inaccurate content. Fortunately there are various monitoring mechanisms, such as required customer registrations and comment approval, that keep contributions in check and maintain the integrity of the content. As with social media channels, community marketing requires a significant investment in time and attention before it can be used effectively. But when managed well, community marketing can be an extremely economical and effective way to build your brand and boost your business.

REAL RESULTS, REAL QUICK

These are all great suggestions for customer profiling, scoring and grading leads, and connecting your marketing automation solution to third-party applications. But how hard is it to get both sales and marketing departments on board and cooperating to implement these suggestions? How long does it actually take to see a real return on these strategies?

Believe it or not, it's really not as hard as it sounds. Selecting a good marketing automation solution is the first step in the process. Once you've implemented the solution and adopted the suggestions discussed above, you'll see results almost immediately.

When a company called Omnipress decided to adopt a marketing automation solution, not only did they achieve their desired results, but they got those results far faster than initially expected. Omnipress offers a "one-stop-shop" solution for producing conference and educational meeting materials in print, digital media, and online formats. Each year, more than 800 associations, meeting professionals, and volunteers trust Omnipress to complete their projects. Omnipress had already developed a robust multichannel marketing plan with an emphasis on providing frequent, compelling content. They were using some programs that provided high-level metrics, but they still lacked in-depth, detailed information about individual visitors. In addition, the marketing team had no established way of passing their findings to their sales team.

Omnipress saw results within just two months of implementing a marketing automation solution. The return far exceeded their expectations. Some of their most noteworthy successes are outlined below:

- Omnipress generated 517% more leads year over year after the adoption of a marketing automation solution.

- They were able to better target the needs of new leads while also gaining valuable insight into the interests, needs, and upgrade potential of current customers.

- Sales reps completely altered their selling approach to one that rarely required cold calling prospects who hadn't already visited the Omnipress website to learn about the company.

- Omnipress kept costs down by using their marketing automation solution to increase incoming leads and to refocus current leads without having to attend expensive trade shows or hire additional sales staff.[12]

If you're willing to abandon the "Dive Bar" approach to lead generation and begin concentrating on quality over quantity, you'll discover that this methodology makes the most of both your marketing and sales assets. If you can create an informed and consistent means of grading and scoring your prospects, coupled with a fair and systematic method of lead assignment, you'll have taken the first big step toward bridging that gap between these notoriously at-odds departments. You'll also find that augmenting your own prospect data with information from outside sources via connectors will greatly enhance the quality of the leads that get passed along to your sales team. A good marketing automation solution with appropriate features makes all of these processes a piece of cake.

Chapter 5. *Staying in Touch*

Once you've profiled your ideal customer and started scoring and grading leads for fit and relevance, you'll find you're getting far better "matches" for your sales team. Now the true courtship can begin. Unfortunately, in today's B2B sales cycle, that courtship can often be long and complicated, and there are lots of opportunities to lose touch along the way.

It's common knowledge that the majority of viable sales leads end up slipping through the cracks. One source suggests that 79% of leads don't get any follow-up from sales because they're perceived to be of below-average quality.[13] Oftentimes, leads that aren't yet ready to buy are dismissed as unviable. But as B2B lead generation expert Brian Carroll has pointed out, with the proper nurturing, as many as 45% of these neglected leads can become sales-ready within just 12 months.[14] Without a system in place to facilitate quick and consistent follow-up, marketers and salespeople unintentionally allow these leads to disappear into a black hole. So what can you do to make sure your company doesn't succumb to these statistics?

LEAD NURTURING

A good marketing automation solution allows you to place non-sales-ready leads into nurturing tracks. You can then ensure that your marketing efforts periodically "touch" them via automated, timed, one-to-one email messages. All links and calls to action in your marketing collateral are tracked individually to prospects, and your sales reps will be notified as soon as a lead responds. By automating the lead nurturing process, you are not only further qualifying your leads, but also freeing up sales or marketing personnel who formerly did this task manually. For your lead nurturing efforts to produce the best results, however, you need to reach out to your prospects in ways that are both sustained *and* timely. In other words, your lead nurturing campaign touches must happen **over time** and **on time**.

OVER TIME: DRIP MARKETING

Drip marketing is a lead nurturing strategy that involves periodically sending out helpful information and relevant promotions to prospects and/or clients. The phrase *drip marketing* is evocative of drip irrigation, the agricultural process of watering plants or crops using small amounts of water over an extended period of time. The idea behind the concept of drip marketing is the "Law of 29", a marketing axiom stating that the average prospect must view a marketing message at least 29 times before they will become a client. While the Law of 29 might not apply in every situation, it is always a good idea to stay in touch with prospects and clients to help build a sustainable working relationship for the long haul. Drip marketing isn't really about selling—it's about building the kind of relationship that will lead to sales down the road.

GET STRATEGIC

The best thing about drip marketing is that it runs itself. Once you put it in place, you don't have to worry about it anymore. Drip marketing does require a plan of action, but you can coordinate with and complement your existing efforts by creating a drip marketing plan that's consistent with your general marketing strategy.

The ideal time to develop drip marketing campaigns is while planning your yearly marketing calendar. Try to send out something at least monthly to keep your name in front of current and prospective clients. Your communications with each group might be different, however. For example, prospects need periodic bits of helpful information that will nudge them to make a buying decision, while current clients should be informed of relevant news such as feature improvements or upgrade opportunities.

Think ahead about possible opportunities for reaching out to prospects and customers in the coming year. These opportunities exist through a wide range of avenues, such as extending invitations to company-sponsored events, passing along industry-specific news, or sharing coverage of your company's annual community outreach activities. For example, you already know months in advance when and where your annual trade show or users conference will take place. Make sure your customers and prospects get an invitation well in advance of the event, followed by timely reminders sent out periodically on a drip program. Marketing automation tools let you create and execute the components of campaigns like these ahead of time so that you'll have more free time to work on fine-tuning other aspects of your marketing strategy.

TONE AND SUBSTANCE

The fundamental underpinnings of any great email campaign—the Four T's—also apply to drip marketing. However, since the goal is not selling but keeping in touch, drip campaigns will be appreciably different in tone and substance. These qualitative differences are reflected in the following collection of best practices for drip marketing.

✓ **Drop the hard sell.** Think of drip marketing items as the Hallmark cards of your marketing toolkit. They're like friendly little notes to remind your prospects and customers that you're thinking of them, that you're keeping their needs in mind, or that you just want to check in to see how they're doing. These greetings can be even more impressive if you're able to tie them to more personal customer interactions by offering holiday greetings, congratulatory wishes at the end of the quarter, or thank-you messages on the anniversary of their signed purchase or service agreement. Sales reps can sign their own communications and, if they wish, include a personal message: *"Hi John, I saw this article and thought you might be interested."*

Marketing automation tools enable this kind of individualized approach through easy personalization of your communications with prospects and customers. Ongoing friendly contact will eventually forge a good working relationship with prospects so that you can drop the hard sell and focus on guiding them to make the buying decision that's in their best interest.

✓ **Get permission.** Back when it passed in 2003, the CAN-SPAM Act (SB877) was jokingly referred to as the "You Can Spam" law. Indeed, many marketers have interpreted it as precisely that—an excuse to send out unsolicited email communications without permission. To comply with the CAN-SPAM Act, marketers need not obtain explicit permission from their intended recipients; there are other ways to comply with the letter, if not the spirit, of the legislation. For years marketers have been using the "negative opt-in" strategy as an effective method for gaining a recipient's unwitting permission to be sent a barrage of emails. This tactic buries a conveniently pre-checked checkbox somewhere on a webpage or in an email. The hope is that the recipient will overlook the checkbox's accompanying language, which effectively grants their "permission" to be emailed in the future.

Such questionable tactics might work in the short term, but in the long run, they will only damage your reputation and undermine your marketing message. If you're serious about relationship marketing, don't even consider taking the covert approach to obtaining permission. Make sure your prospects are only getting emails that they actually want to receive.

✓ **Send presents.** Just as any human courtship can be sweetened by the occasional bouquet of flowers or little memento, so can customer relationships. Marketing automation solutions make it easy to deliver genuine value in your communications by making presents of your presence. You need only ensure that your message is useful, unique, and not blatantly promotional.

Opportunities for clever gift-giving are limited only by the imagination. Nurturing emails can include links to short customer testimonial videos and case studies; articles, reports, and white papers; industry-related news or relevant third-party information; and, best of all, freebies such as basic consulting services, free sample chapters of your upcoming book, special product sneak previews, or helpful proprietary tips and tricks.

✓ **Balance variety and consistency.** You definitely want prospects to recognize your brand and to identify with your marketing slogans, but you don't want to become boring, redundant, or irrelevant. There's some truth in that old saw about familiarity breeding contempt. Your brand can be consistent from drip to drip without making your prospect think, *"Didn't I just see this last week?"* Blasting away at your prospects with duplicate emails, or emails that are so similar as to seem like duplicates, is not marketing—it's harassment.

✓ **Segment your lists.** If you interact with different types of prospects, think about their specific needs and interests and make your messaging relevant. This kind of specialization will most likely require using more than one nurturing track. You could decide to segment your leads based on any number of distinguishing factors, such as a prospect's job title or industry, or the products in which they're interested. Then make sure to follow up with targeted content that each grouping of prospects will find relevant or beneficial. Using rules features in your marketing automation platform makes it easy to create segmented nurturing lists.

✓ **Be patient (but not lazy).** Teach your sales team to be patient—but not lazy. Drip marketing is a great tool to keep your company and product top of mind with prospects, but it can't take the place of traditional sales calls. Conversely, your sales team has to let marketing plant the seed and build the relationship before they send a sales rep in with guns blazing.

The bottom line? Leads that aren't ready to buy don't want to talk to salespeople. That's why drip marketing is such a powerful tool. There are plenty of sales opportunities out there, and each one can take months to develop. Rather than having the sales team jump on every opportunity with equal vigor, you should task your marketing team with passing on only the most sales-ready leads. The remaining prospects should be nurtured, slowly but surely, until they're ready to buy.

Many B2B products and services are complex,

requiring potential clients to do a significant amount of research before they're ready to buy. Drip marketing is a great way to do this, because marketers can customize the information that each lead receives, making sure that this information is sent out at regular intervals. Obviously, drip marketing can do most of the heavy lifting for you here, but always keep in mind that trying to sell to leads too early in the sales cycle is risky and usually ends up being counterproductive since nobody wants to feel like they're being pushed to buy before they're ready. On the other hand, having the sales team manually nurture leads is a waste of time. Salespeople should be able to spend their time doing what they do best: selling the product to leads that already know what your product is about, and persuading these leads that your product is the best fit for their needs. Drip marketing lets the sales team concentrate on selling by ensuring that marketing is creating high-quality leads that are both a good fit and are ready to buy.

One of the key benefits of marketing automation is the coordination it fosters between sales and marketing teams. This kind of teamwork is critical to creating a seamless sales cycle that begins with a carefully designed marketing strategy (including drip marketing campaigns) and ends with a salesperson closing the deal. Because drip marketing isn't about hard selling, it doesn't make the sale on its own. However, it helps build a positive relationship with prospects, who are then nurtured until they're ready to buy.

✓ **Think outside the inbox.** Drip emails are the backbone of any drip marketing strategy, but there are other ways to communicate in the context of a drip campaign. Other options for making regular contact with your prospects include sending handwritten notes, leaving unintrusive voicemails, and making the most of social media outlets for periodic messages.

✓ **Don't leave customers behind.** Just because some of your leads haven't been converted into opportunities yet doesn't mean that they have no value. In fact, some of them might just be waiting to hear from you. Setting up a drip marketing program specifically designed with old leads in mind will ensure that even if your sales reps don't stay in touch, your nurturing efforts will. Whatever happened to that lead who dropped off the radar because a sales rep wasn't able to make contact? What about those unconverted website visitors who signed up for a webinar but never showed up? You were once top of mind for these prospects. At some point, you did something right that got their attention. Don't sacrifice the hard work you've already invested and the relationship you've started to develop with them. Marketing automation tools make it easy and economical to reengage these leads, and when the time comes, drip marketing can greatly reduce the time that sales reps must spend in reiterating the benefits of your product or service. Maintaining constant contact means that potential customers won't slip through the cracks.

ON TIME: RESPONSIVE MARKETING

In the last chapter, we discussed some suggestions for optimal timing of emails with regard to the day of the week or time of day. But because it applies to building the customer relationship, lead nurturing requires a special sense of timing. To market responsively, you need to consider the experience of the typical recipient who joins your list, signs up for that first webinar, or otherwise enters into a relationship with your company. What will the significant milestones in that emerging relationship be? And how at each milestone can you best respond both rapidly and appropriately?

The emerging customer relationship actually takes shape much as a dating relationship would. From the point of introduction, the relationship progresses—sometimes slowly, sometimes quickly—through the initial "getting acquainted" stage before finally maturing into a committed relationship built on trust. In the context of today's complex sales cycle, that progress might not always be as fast or linear as expected, but marketing technology tools can help you keep in touch throughout the entire process, ensuring that your budding relationship with a prospective customer never lapses or breaks down.

The Introduction

The original touchpoint in any relationship is the initial meeting—that one chance you have to make a good first impression. The welcome message is probably the most widely read email in any given drip program, and it's crucial in that it comes at a time when new subscribers have recently become acquainted with your company or product and are highly receptive to receiving your message. Yet many marketers still manage to miss this golden opportunity to say *Hello*, *Welcome*, or *It's nice to meet you*. A benchmark study published by Smith-Harmon in 2009 found some surprising results. Out of 112 of the largest online retailers surveyed:

- Only 76% sent out welcome emails
- 23% took longer than 24 hours to send out a welcome message after subscribers signed up
- Only 76% explained the benefits of being a subscriber
- Only 87% included a link to their homepage.[15]

It's mystifying that so many marketers still manage to botch, or completely miss out on, this once-in-a-business-relationship opportunity, particularly since welcome emails typically generate substantial open and click-through rates. Marketing automation tools can be invaluable in helping you nail this decisive opportunity for each and every prospect you come in contact with.

Welcome emails can set expectations by informing recipients of what they might encounter in future messages. They can be designed as one or two simple messages, or a series of notifications. They should be tailored to reflect the specific nature of your introduction; for example, prospects who sign up to receive a newsletter should be thanked specifically for doing so, while those who join an online user community should get a customized *Welcome to our community!*-type message. If your introduction has been through a referral, this should be acknowledged, and the prospect should be placed in the appropriate campaign. The bottom line is that any campaign strategy needs to recognize, and accord the proper respect to, that all-important first meeting. First impressions are important. It's critical to get things right the first time, or there might not be a second time.

Getting Acquainted

In the middle stage of a developing relationship, the two

parties are getting to know one another. You've learned something about your new prospect from information he or she has voluntarily provided, and your lead scoring and grading tools are working behind the scenes to gauge their fit and their interest level based on their activities online. But your prospect is learning about you in this stage, too. When prospects are in exploratory mode, they are seeking information, evaluating your products or services against those of your competitors, and absorbing cues about how you might treat them in an established customer relationship. This intermediate stage is brimming with opportunities for educating prospects, building personal relationships, and gently nudging prospects toward that all-important commitment: the sale.

For a drip marketing campaign to be really effective at this stage, it needs to respond rapidly to every overture your prospect makes, and every response should be as relevant as possible. It is at this stage that you can most effectively employ marketing automation tools for prospect nurturing. Using tracking clues from a prospect's online activity, you can engineer your communications to deliver information with increasing relevancy based on where he or she is in the buying process. This can be especially important with regard to big-ticket items that require many weeks or months of research on the part of potential buyers.

B2B marketing strategist Ardath Albee recommends

creating a storyline to help keep marketing content consistently tied to your main message. This involves creating personas for your most ideal prospect segments and then building a storyline for each persona, detailing possible routes to purchase for each product or solution so that you can map content to buying stages. The goal is to deliver a continuous flow of content that matches up to prospect needs from the start.[16]

This approach obviously requires more forethought and planning than just the basic drip marketing approach of sending content over time. It implies the creation of a more complex rule structure within your marketing automation platform, which requires you to develop a repository of generic content to send off at each stage of the buying process. Having a marketing automation solution in place simplifies this complex task by letting you craft a conceptually sophisticated plan that can be implemented simply and automatically. For example, a request for a white paper can be acknowledged by an autoresponder email that supplies the appropriate link. If the prospect does not click the white paper link in the email, a follow-up email is automatically sent two days later with a note asking if they've had a chance to read the white paper and providing a link to see it again. This process can be repeated every so often, but with related white papers, case studies, or other relevant material. You'll be able to monitor prospect responses throughout this entire process so that sales reps will be able to swiftly respond to prospect needs with appropriate personal attention.

It's Not Over Yet

In the third stage of building a customer relationship, you and your prospect are now a team—you've committed to working together and have officially become an item. Now that your prospect is a customer, it might seem like the relationship has ended, or perhaps that it more properly belongs to service and support. But this is not the time for marketing to quietly slip out of the room.

As drip marketing expert Lori Feldman (a.k.a. "The Database Diva") has pointed out, new customers can often suffer from buyer's remorse. It's just human nature for customers to wonder if maybe, just maybe, they should have shopped around a little more, negotiated harder for a better deal, or asked a few more questions. "That's a disconnect," Feldman says, "and the only way to fix it is to overload a new customer with personalized attention through an automated onboarding process."[17] This is a great idea, not only because it continues to nurture the customer, but also because it adds ongoing value to the relationship by ensuring that your new customer has everything they need to succeed with your company—and, by extension, no nagging regrets.

The "sold" customer shouldn't be forgotten or written off simply as an opportunity marked as "won" in the CRM. Current customers are often sources of repeat business or referrals, so it's crucial to maintain a good relationship with them even after the initial deal has been closed. Even if your customers are not especially susceptible to up-selling or cross-selling, it always pays to cultivate references and advocates—someone who feels so positively about your company and their experience with your product or service that they're willing to provide great references for future customers. What do satisfied customers typically do when they have a great experience? They tell their friends and colleagues. The huge payoff of a drip campaign that stays in touch with satisfied customers beyond the final stage of the buying cycle is more than worth the minimal effort it takes to set it up within your marketing automation platform.

There are plenty of chances at this stage to say *thank you*—something that few companies really take the time to do for their customers—as well as many opportunities for follow-up campaign items. Just as you wouldn't miss the opportunity to follow up after a great date or business meeting, you don't want to squander the chance to send a direct response to a prospect who has downloaded a white paper, participated in a webinar, watched a demonstration, or signed up for a free trial. Automated email campaigns can also be used to supplement any follow-up calls by sales reps during this end stage.

A FINAL WORD ON DRIP MARKETING

The goals of a drip marketing campaign can extend beyond lead nurturing to provide additional value to your marketing team. The resultant outcomes can be not only specific, but also measurable. Email open, click-through, and opt-out rates are some examples of useful drip marketing metrics. You can look at these early-stage metrics, in addition to late-stage ones such as time to purchase and purchase frequency, in order to get an idea of how effective your drip marketing campaigns are and to calculate ROI for specific tools.

Setting up a drip marketing campaign requires an initial commitment of time and planning, but this investment pays off many times over. According to marketing research firm Forrester Research, companies that excel at drip marketing raise their win rates by 7% and have sales representatives who make quota 9% more often. Additionally, prospects and customers who receive drip marketing messages buy more, require less discounting, and have shorter sales cycles than those who were not part of a drip campaign.[18] In today's business climate, even modest improvements like these can constitute an important competitive edge. If you're not leveraging marketing automation tools to keep prospects and customers engaged through carefully crafted lead nurturing efforts, you're effectively leaving revenue on the table.

Chapter 6. Making the Most of What You've Got

Aside from your company's vital intellectual property and human capital, your most valuable assets are your website and customer database. Marketing automation was initially developed to help companies make the most of those important assets, enabling them to wring every bit of useful data from prospect interaction with their webpages in the hopes that capturing better intelligence would generate more qualified leads. This is a tall order, but plenty of companies have adopted marketing automation solutions that regularly deliver on these goals.

But that's not the whole story. In a cyclical, reiterative progression, marketing automation solutions use prospect data to continually refine the lead generation process, showing you how to build even better webpages, how to optimize your marketing campaigns, and how to get even better prospect data. Better data yields better prospects in greater numbers, which feeds back into a continuously improving lead generation strategy.

This chapter will explain how this cycle of continuous refinement works. It will also outline some of the common mistakes and worst practices that prevent marketers from getting the greatest value from their websites and data.

THE COMPANY WEBSITE

Conventional wisdom holds that a company's homepage will be the page that visitors land on most frequently. This is an assumption worth examining, but for now it's fair to say that while every company *has* a homepage, very few actually do a good job of converting traffic from it.

THE HOMEPAGE

The typical corporate homepage provides dozens of links, some sort of lifestyle image in a banner, and either no call to action or too many calls to action. Lots of digital real estate is occupied by company history, mission statements, and explanations of corporate values. But in the rush to provide as much information and as many options as possible, the traditional homepage frequently alienates visitors, leaving them overwhelmed and possibly confused.

This isn't a book about web design; there are plenty of other resources out there already for that. This guide is for

B2B marketers looking for better ways to generate and nurture quality leads for their sales teams. Even so, experience has shown that there are some pretty consistent reasons as to why marketers fail to capitalize on this valuable asset, even allowing their homepage to hinder, rather than help, the sales effort. Some of the most common mistakes marketers make with regard to their corporate website's homepage are outlined below.

✘ **Too much clutter.** Prospects who have come to your site through search or referral have come there for a specific reason. Odds are that it's not to decide whether to buy stock in the company. Your founding partners were most certainly wonderful people. Your mission statement is probably quite inspiring. But if a prospect has come to your homepage seeking information on a specific product or service—that is, if they actually want to *buy* something from you—they need to see a clear path to achieve this goal immediately upon arriving on your site. Dozens of links, vague jargon-laden copy, and meaningless lifestyle images are not merely confusing—they're direct obstacles to that goal.

   Ideally, your homepage should aim to do no more than provide clear top-level navigation to relevant landing pages with appropriate copy. But if your homepage must do more than this, try to keep it as simple and clean as possible. You want a scannable layout with short paragraphs, bolded subheadings, and bulleted lists. Concentrate on one primary call to action (download a demo, sign up for a webinar, etc.) that encompasses the single key thing that you hope each your site's visitors will do. If you have secondary calls to action, keep them smaller and format them with a different design element, such as a different color or button style.

✖ **Not segmenting the audience.** The most valuable work that your homepage can do is to allow visitors to quickly self-select the buyer persona that most closely resembles them, as this is where you have the greatest chance for conversion. For example, the audience might be classified by persona into IT person, business analyst, or executive decision-maker. Once you've assigned a persona to a given visitor, marketing automation tools can create a unique profile and serve call-outs that are specific to that persona. Another benefit of persona segmentation is that interior page content and navigation menus can be tailored to the audience, and by tracking these specialized page views, you can capture even more actionable data than you could by just keeping track of general page views. Segmenting your audience from the very first time they reach your homepage will optimize the performance of your marketing automation tools.

✖ **Not providing contact information.** There's just no excuse for this one. Burying or omitting your contact info, email address, and phone number is just not helpful for lead generation. Every page in your site should have your contact information displayed in a consistent and conspicuous location. Inexplicably, a surprising number of companies omit such details from their homepages. What's worse, this grievous error or omission has become common practice for companies that spend considerable resources driving traffic to their homepage. Don't be shy. Put your contact information out there for all to see. It's the best way to get interested prospects in touch with you.

✖ **Design flaws that encourage drop-off.** Most site content simply ends at the bottom of the page, leaving the reader to scroll back up to the top, click the back button in the browser, or possibly move on to a different website. Make sure you have a call to action at the bottom of each page, even if it's just a text link to other areas of your site. If you're linking off your site to partner sites or related articles, set the link to open in a new tab or window to avoid losing the visitor.

✖ **Letting content go stale.** Old content can be a serious embarrassment for your company. The pictures from last year's trade show, "featured" blog posts that are months old, headlines about expired promotions, and links to last quarter's newsletter or to unused landing pages not only create noise in search engines, but are also a major turn-off for visitors to your site. Ferret out that expired content—everywhere on your website, but especially where it appears on your homepage—and either properly archive it, or get rid of it altogether. Your site needs to have consistently fresh content to attract a steady stream of visitors.

✖ **Wasting precious taglines.** B2B services and products can be quite complex, so it can be hard to summarize a website's purpose in a concise tagline that's short enough for visitors to skim quickly and understand. Unfortunately, the challenge of coming up with a compelling tagline leads many businesses to tag their homepages with meaningless strings of nebulous buzzword-filled expressions, such as *"leveraging the power of convergence"* or *"robust solutions for today's business."* These empty word strings say nothing about what your product or service actually is or does, and they do nothing to distinguish your page or company from a world of others.

Don't be afraid to say what you do or tell what you

sell. If yours is the type of business that would benefit from geographic convenience or a hometown boost, you might also want to consider localizing your homepage tag. At the very least, don't waste the search value of your homepage tag completely. Remember, too, that the page title will be the default entry when users bookmark your site as a Favorite. If you don't want the bookmark to read, "*Welcome to the home of...*", you should alphabetize and tag accordingly.

LANDING PAGES

The previous section emphasized the importance of a good homepage. But today's web has produced one apparent contradiction: There's really no such thing as a homepage anymore. Search engines have turned this notion of the be-all-end-all homepage on its head because they rank unique webpages, not websites. As Google Analytics guru Avinash Kaushik frequently says, there's no longer any "golden door" through which all of your visitors will pass. Every page of your website should be looked upon as a point of entry into your website. Every page should have quality content that optimizes prospect conversion opportunities. Give each and every visitor multiple chances to answer your site's calls to action.

In web parlance, any page to which a visitor is directed after clicking an advertisement or an email link is termed a *landing page.* While the term is relative and might actually *be* the company's homepage, increasingly these days it's not. A landing page generally displays content that is specific to the advertisement, search keyword, or clicked link. Driving visitors directly to your homepage can be an ineffective method of converting prospects because they are simply presented with too many choices. On the other hand, a landing page offers a streamlined path designed to elicit a specific action by the visitor. Homepages may remain relatively static, but landing pages can be virtual chameleons, constantly changing their content based on specific promotions and seasonal offers, as well as making the improvements that ongoing testing and tracking reveal.

One of the greatest strengths of marketing automation is that it enables the creation of campaign-specific dedicated landing pages without requiring any coding. A WYSIWYG graphical interface allows you to drag and drop elements into the header, content, or footer sections of your landing page and to easily format your page using HTML, rich text, built-in image hosting, and other formatting options to match the look and feel of your brand. These custom landing pages can be easily tested by non-technical users.

"An improved landing page can result in an average 40% increase in conversion."

Stefan Tornquist, Research Director, MarketingSherpa

Boosting landing page conversion

For B2B marketers with long and complex sales cycles, conversion typically involves getting a visitor to fill out a form in exchange for something of value: a white paper, a demo, or a free consultation, for example. But there are four distinct groups of people interacting with your landing pages upon whom you're banking for that conversion:

- Visitors who leave within 10 seconds of arriving at your landing page. These make up the vast majority of viewers.

- Visitors who leave when they decide your landing page is not sufficiently compelling. This is the next largest segment.

- Visitors who attempt to fill out your form, but fail or give up and then drop off.

- Visitors who successfully convert to become leads.

As the list suggests, online visitors are busy and easily distracted, so the odds for conversion are usually stacked against you. But there are a number of steps that you can take to boost the effectiveness of your landing pages and to improve those odds significantly. Some of these steps are simple best practices. Others have been made possible by recently developed web technologies. But all of these suggestions will increase the value of your web assets and contribute directly to your online lead generation program.

✓ **Reinforce the keyword correspondence.** It's all well and good if your target keyword brings a prospect to your page, but you still have to get them to convert. An easy way to start optimizing your landing pages for conversion is to make sure your headlines and images speak directly to the corresponding keywords. If a prospect has clicked on an ad about *email marketing*, make sure the page they land on is about email marketing and not just a general page with your company logo.

✓ **Skip the lifestyle shots.** How many times have you gone to a landing page and been greeted with a header graphic that has nothing to do with the offer presented? Do images like a businessman with a laptop or a girl flying a kite really have anything to do with the white paper you are about to request? Probably not. A better approach is to provide a sneak peak of the promised content, such as a small image of the white paper or demo that you're offering. This "hero shot" gives your visitors something tangible to look forward to and offers a much more compelling reason to convert.

✓ **Keep it above the fold.** You have tons of great content and fantastic visuals. Save those for your homepage. Your landing page should be a quick, clean path to conversion for visitors. Eliminate as much scrolling as possible by keeping most, if not all, of your content above the fold. This axiom was true for newspaper advertising and it is every bit as true for the web.

✓ **Lay out your value proposition.** Your conversion rate will improve significantly when you're able to answer clearly, and in detail, the *"What's in it for me?"* question that's in the back of all of our minds as we check out new websites. Don't make a guessing game out of your value proposition. If your Buyer's Guide contains (1) a five-page overview, (2) a 100-point checklist of what to look for, (3) a 20-point vendor comparison, and (4) an ROI calculator, then by all means, say so! Conversions are much more likely when prospects know exactly what they're getting.

✓ **Brag about your credibility.** Visitors who are not familiar with your company may be hesitant to enter their contact information on your site, even in exchange for something of value. Displaying a few third-party credibility indicators or the seals, certifications, and awards that your company has earned can go a long way in helping to build trust with your visitors. Examples include client feedback and testimonials; site security badges like VeriSign, Thawte, and TRUSTe; ratings from the Better Business Bureau or similar organizations; or any other industry recognitions that your company may have received. Badges such as the Inc. 500 and Marketing Excellence Awards reassure visitors that your company is legitimate and that their information is safe. They also serve as the first step to establishing your brand's reputation with new visitors.

✓ **Provide assurance of your ethics.** It's always a good idea to include a short privacy statement that ensures prospects that their email address or other information will not be abused or re-sold. It's comforting to see a prominently displayed statement along the lines of *"We take your privacy seriously and will never share your contact information."* This is a small step, but it can help reassure prospects who may be hesitant to provide their information.

✓ **Lock up some content.** When a visitor submits a form, many companies simply redirect them to the requested content, be it an article, a white paper, or a demo. A better approach is to clearly set the expectation that you will email a link to the white paper or demo upon form submission. While this does not always guarantee that the lead will give you a valid business email address, it does increase the likelihood. Create this expectation by including a straightforward statement such as *"Please complete the form below to have the white paper emailed to you."*

Using validation on forms allows you to set custom levels of approval to ensure that the email addresses that are entered are not from free providers (often important for B2B marketing), come from a valid email domain, or both. Marketing automation vendors and other quality form hosting providers can actually check the email domain in real-time and display a gentle error message if the validation conditions are not met. When delivering the promised content via email, it's best to send a link to the document's location, rather than sending the document as an attachment. This allows for tracking link click-throughs to determine exactly when the materials were accessed, or if they were even accessed at all. When your sales reps follow up with a phone call, they will benefit much more from knowing when the document was likely read rather than when the email was opened.

Even if you don't have a large library of locked-down content to offer your prospects, providing links to other sections of your website can help you continue tracking your visitors to gain additional insight into their level of interest. Additionally, including links in the email you send your prospects once they've completed a form will provide you with yet another opportunity to reengage those prospects who have already left your site.

✓ **Give some content away.** MarketingSherpa cites a case study of a company called INTTRA that took a new approach to forms—a voluntary approach. INTTRA was dealing with a very traditional industry segment with prospects who were more resistant than most with regard to filling out a form in order to view a product demo. Instead of requiring registration, INTTRA decided to allow anyone to view the demo but still provided a form in a sidebar for those who wanted more information.

Despite adopting such an unconventional approach, INTTRA ended up with a surprisingly good conversion rate. Their statistics revealed that 23% of prospects who viewed the demo also filled out the form. Upon converting, these prospects received an autoresponder email that included additional resources, and especially promising leads were passed on to the sales team as appropriate. These leads were obviously qualified since they were actively seeking information.[19]

We use a similar technique on our company website. After viewing a free demo that does not require registration, visitors can click a *Test Drive* button that takes them to a conversion form. This strategy yields a good conversion rate because it makes it so easy for prospects to take the next step towards conversion.

Even though it goes against conventional wisdom, it's still worth considering the notion of having content on your site that isn't locked down behind a form. It can be a good way to ensure that you are capturing the maximum amount of qualified leads and making the process pain-free for your prospects.

✓ **Get smart about forms.** Forms are your lifeline to your prospects. They're valuable tools that let you collect crucial prospect data so that, once qualified, you can funnel those prospects into the sales pipeline. Typically, prospects visit a website and can only look around so long before they're confronted with that dreaded form asking them to provide more information if they wish to proceed. This is a make-or-break moment in that if the prospect doesn't yet see enough value, he or she won't be persuaded to divulge such details and will abandon the form (and probably your website, too).

Think about the last time this happened to you. You Googled something and clicked on what looked like a promising link, only to encounter a daunting form asking for a whole lot of info after you'd browsed just a few pages on the site. Either the form was too long and tedious to bother filling out, or it asked you for far more information than you were comfortable providing.

"Why is it asking for my mother's maiden name?!" you asked incredulously, promptly clicking back to try a different search result. You made a quick cost-benefit calculation that the tradeoff (your mother's maiden name in exchange for a view of the page you wanted to see) wasn't worth it, and you abandoned the form and navigated away from that site, possibly forever.

You obviously don't want the same outcome with visitors to your own site. You want them to come in and have a look around, be dazzled by what you have to offer, and gladly give up a few bits of personal data in exchange for the multitude of benefits your site so clearly provides. Make sure you don't lose them at this critical juncture! Remember that, just like you, your prospects are also prone to form abandonment. But you can help them work through their abandonment issues by designing simple, un-intimidating forms that they don't mind filling out.

Here are some best practices for reducing form abandonment:

✓ **Don't waste your visitor's time.** Don't make your visitors repeat themselves in the same form, and don't ask them for the same piece of information more than once. Whenever possible, use time savers like drop-downs and checkboxes that don't require prospects to craft their own response (more on this below). This approach also makes it much easier for you to aggregate data and automate processes on the back end.

✓ **Minimize the required fields.** Nothing is more frustrating for most visitors than arriving on a landing page and seeing a massive form with most or all of its fields marked with the "required field" red asterisk of death. Companies that ask visitors to fill in more than a handful of fields in the first interaction are just encouraging drop-off. B2B sales cycles by their very nature are often multi-touch and complex, and each touchpoint provides another opportunity to collect data, which means that marketers have more time to compile prospect profiles. Why risk alienating prospects by rushing to get everything up front?

✓ **Use progressive profiling.** Using conditional fields allows you to progressively build an in-depth prospect profile by asking for just one or two data points during each prospect interaction, depending on the information they've already provided.

Picture this: A visitor hits your landing page and is asked for her name, email address, and company in exchange for a white paper. Twenty minutes later, she requests a flash demo and is asked for her job title. In three weeks, she returns to your site and is asked for her department in exchange for a case study. A few days later, she is asked about her buying stage after requesting a live demonstration. This is an unintrusive and non-threatening way to collect crucial data, bit by bit, until you have a complete representation of this prospect and her buying intentions.

The same form is used for all the content across your site, but progressive profiling allows the form to intelligently display only the fields you're missing for that particular prospect. Marketing automation tools employ cookies to identify returning prospects and remember what information these prospects have already provided. Forms with progressive profiling features allow you to set up tiers in advance so that each time a prospect returns, they will be asked the appropriate questions. Try to keep the first form down to four fields at the most, and guide prospects to view other compelling content across your site in order to gradually obtain additional data from them.

✓ **Tone down your error messages.** In terms of the top website visitor annoyances, harsh in-your-face error messages come a close second to lengthy forms. Imagine that your visitor has taken the time to fill out and submit a form in order to receive your white paper. Instead of the satisfying *"Thank you"* message she expects to pop up, she's greeted with a glaring red error message—or worse, an empty form that forces her to start all over again. Guess what? Chances are, she won't bother.

The quick fix for this common issue is to handle error validation instantly. Your forms should be configured to display an error message as soon as a visitor fails to correctly complete the required field. For example, if a visitor is filling out a form and enters an invalid state abbreviation, make sure that your form immediately displays a corresponding prompt: *"Please enter a valid state."* This warning is immediate but much more subtle, and it's preferable in that it allows your visitor to correct entries without losing the data they've already provided, reducing the risk of form abandonment.

✓ **Test, test, and test again.** The one great truth about landing pages is that you can always improve upon them with testing. Marketing automation platforms usually allow you to set up a simple multivariate test, which automatically distributes your incoming traffic to two separate landing pages. The landing pages should be very similar, perhaps varying only very slightly in design, copy, or content. Eventually you'll be able to evaluate which variation has a higher conversion rate, which will help you develop the most effective landing page possible. But don't stop here. You should continually test and refine landing pages because there's always room for improvement, especially when you have good data.

At a loss as to which landing page attributes you should be testing? Try experimenting with a few of the following variables:

- **Headline** – Keep it short and compelling; the headline should always convey an immediate benefit to the reader.

- **Offer** – Experiment with offering a variety of incentives (white papers, free consultations, demos, and other motivating content) to find out what prospects view as most valuable.

- **Visuals** – Try using compelling "sneak peek" shots of your white paper cover, an internal page, or a demo screenshot to stimulate additional interest in your offerings.

- **Form length** – If you started with a lengthy form, try removing a few required fields and see if your conversion rate improves.

- **Form fields** – Try substituting fields (e.g., *department* vs. *job title*) or changing up formatting by adding more user-friendly features like drop-down menus and checkboxes.

Although testing can be difficult and tedious to carry out manually, marketing automation solutions can make complex tests a breeze by automatically assigning traffic to each of your page designs and reporting on the results.

Whatever your need for forms may be, marketing automation solutions simplify the form-building process through an intuitive drag-and-drop interface. Because forms are so easy to create, they become an organic and flexible source for getting clean, accurate, relevant prospect data—which is what you *really* want from the investment you've made in your company's website and landing pages.

GETTING VALUE FROM YOUR DATA

If you're considering a marketing automation solution for inbound lead generation, you are probably most excited about the vast *quantity* of data you can collect on prospects and their needs. But you can also greatly enhance the *quality* of this data by utilizing your marketing automation platform as a data cleaner. And there's plenty of incentive for keeping that data clean. According to B2B marketing strategist Ardath Albee, the revenue lift that will result from merely cleaning up dirty prospect data can be as great as 70%.[20]

KEEPING IT CLEAN

While CRM systems perform many functions effectively, deduplication of prospect data does not seem to be one of them. To keep your CRM data clean in terms of the leads that come from your website, take these important steps:

✓ **Automatically check for duplicates in existing data.** Prospects can enter your CRM through many different ways—through filling out forms, dropping by your booth at trade shows, subscribing to newsletters, and so on. Most companies don't check their CRM to see if the prospect is already there. But the same person filling out several forms, or completing one form multiple times, can create unwanted noise in your database. Funneling all of your leads through a marketing automation platform before they enter your CRM will match records based on criteria like email address in order to distinguish new records from duplicates.

✓ **Get data validation at the form level.** At a minimum, you should ensure that email addresses are in a valid format (*blank@site.com*) before letting them enter your database. An even better approach is setting up your form to ping the domain in real time to ensure that it has an actual mail exchange record. This latter method prevents prospects from entering an invalid address such as *abcdef@abcdef.com*, which would pass the first test. You could take this one step further by actually refusing to accept addresses from free email providers. Generally speaking, you don't want sales reps to waste time following up with prospects that supplied Yahoo!, Hotmail, or Gmail addresses.

For a visitor whose email address fails validation, be sure to provide a soft error message as soon as they tab off the field, as opposed to having them click the submit button, only to be surprised by a glaring error notification. This simple step will discourage drop-off among legitimate prospects while still weeding out unsuitable leads from your screening process.

✓ **Limit choices via drop-downs instead of free-form text.** Using drop-down lists or menus and other structured data fields like checkboxes is a great way to standardize your data while streamlining the visitor experience. This practice makes prospect data fields like industry and job title much more usable later, as it helps you avoid permutations of the same title (e.g., *VP*, *Vice President*, etc.). Predefined field values result in better, cleaner data for you. And because forms can be filled out much faster than with free text fields, they waste less visitor time, contributing to the likelihood that your prospects will offer up what is asked of them.

✓ **Keep bots away with built-in spam prevention**. If left unchecked, bots can quickly fill a company's database with gibberish. Many companies (including Google) stop bots in their tracks by using *captchas*, an additional field where you enter a string of text or a number to prove that you are indeed a human. Captchas, while effective in term of spam prevention, can frustrate visitors and drive down your conversion rate, so you may want to consider using a hidden spam trap that humans will never need to see or deal with.

Each of these techniques can be accomplished either through custom programming or via a good marketing automation solution. Either way, the technology is out there, and taking these precautions will make your life easier by keeping your data cleaner.

ACTIVITY TRACKING

While 99% of web analytics programs collect information at the macro level, the analytics tools built into marketing automation solutions track traffic at the individual or micro level. Advanced prospect activity tracking allows you to view a log of every touchpoint with your prospect. You can see the pages your prospect has visited, find out which files they've downloaded, keep track of email correspondence, and more. Additionally, tracking tools record all activities that occurred prior to the prospect's conversion. With this information, you can nurture leads much more efficiently and help your sales team close more deals. As prospects interact with your website, their scores will increase, promoting the most active prospects to the top of the follow-up list.

TRACK ANONYMOUS VISITORS

Although most B2B marketers would love to follow up with all of the visitors to your website, the majority of traffic will unfortunately be anonymous. Some studies have shown that as few as 2% of website visitors actually become viable prospects. Wouldn't it be helpful if you could somehow track the other 98% of these visitors? Marketing automation can help you do that, too.

A good marketing automation solution can record abandoned or updated data from a form that wasn't submitted. Suppose that your anonymous visitor tracking shows that a prospect entered three different email addresses before successfully completing the form. He first entered a Yahoo! address and was prompted to use a non-free address. He then tried to give a made-up address and was prompted to give a valid email. He finally broke down and entered his corporate email address. This sort of scenario might indicate that this prospect is wary of being contacted via email. It might be more appropriate to put leads like this on a nurturing track rather than contacting them immediately with a sales pitch.

Tracking your website's visitors, even the anonymous ones, can tell you much more than you might think. Being able to track at the individual prospect level is like playing detective with anonymous visitors to your website and can greatly improve your use of marketing automation. Here's what you can learn with the click of a mouse:

- **IP address.** Some marketing automation solutions can use a visitor's IP address to find out what company or organization is visiting your site. Often the IP address doesn't provide much value, as it comes from a generic internet service provider (ISP). But a small percentage, (usually 0.5–10%) of IP addresses can be identified at the company level; these are primarily mid-size and large companies (hospitals, government entities, and institutions of higher education) that have their own connectivity (T1 or T3 line). Marketing automation tools can easily identify visitors from such companies, and once you know this, you can have your sales team act on that information accordingly.

- **Browser and OS.** People who use Firefox are typically

more tech-savvy than those who use Internet Explorer. Mac and Linux users are a distinguished category for companies selling technology products or services.

- **Hostname/Referrer.** The most informative field within this feature is the Hostname/Referrer, which tells you the origin of a visitor, including their IP address and the name under which it's registered. From a marketing standpoint, tracking patterns of anonymous visitors can help you identify trends in particular industry verticals and potential new audiences for your product or service. From a sales perspective, this information has several uses. If you're in the middle of the sales cycle, knowing that there have been numerous visits originating from a company that's evaluating your product gives a good indication as to just how serious they are. This information can also be useful in helping salespeople locate appropriate contacts at a prospective client company.

- **Search origination.** Knowing which search engine (Yahoo, Google, Bing, etc.) brought a particular visitor to your site can help you determine where your best leads are coming from and in what proportions, thereby improving allocation of your marketing spend.

- **Page views and interaction time.** Analyzing page views and interaction time metrics allow you to see exactly which components of your site each individual prospect has been browsing and for how long. This tells you what things are most (and least) important to potential customers, allowing you to customize your lead nurturing strategy and tailor your sales pitch accordingly. Page views and interaction time can also be good indicators of whether or not your page design is meeting your expectations for providing useful, coherent content to a particular market segment or prospect persona.

- **Search term.** The nature of a search—that is, which search terms brought the searcher to your site—can tell you a great deal about how serious a particular visitor might be. If a visitor searches for the answer to a very general question (*"What is marketing automation?"*), they may or may not be worth pursuing. If they're searching for your product by name, however, you can bet that they're interested in your product and didn't just happen upon your site by chance. Knowing the specific search phrases people use to find your site can provide a wealth of information that quantitative examinations of conversion rates just can't convey. This knowledge also enables you to better optimize your pages based on popular keywords for determining which campaigns are most effective.

WITH GREAT POWER COMES GREAT RESPONSIBILITY

The information gleaned from the advanced tracking features built into most marketing automation solutions can put you in a powerful position—one you can use to great advantage during the sales process. But it's important to use this information wisely. Though most people are aware of the ability to track activities online, some might still be averse to the idea of being tracked themselves. The first time you call a prospect within a few minutes of their visiting your website, they may brush it off as a coincidence. If you call them within a few minutes of every single visit, they might start to feel a little bit intimidated. It's crucial to make sure that you and your sales team are on the same page about how much immediate follow-up is too much.

The one exception to this guideline is when someone requests immediate follow-up, as with a support form or a contact form. In these cases, a fast response time would be interpreted positively. Marketing automation tools can give you a jump-start by sending you alerts; some platforms even incorporate web-to-phone technology that instantly connects sales and services representatives to incoming prospects by phone as soon as a request is submitted. As a general rule, simply keep in mind that when calling on prospects you should use your insider knowledge to wow

them with a personalized pitch, not to scare them by
coming on too strong.

Think Outside the Inbox

Try driving visitors to landing pages, tracked files, or unique
URLs to measure clicks on materials you post through Twitter,
Facebook, or other social media channels.

WINNING THE SEO ARMS RACE

Search engine optimization (SEO) has become the arms
race of the internet age. Getting high placement in search
results through the best page rankings is the prize that's
perpetually just beyond reach, and companies will do
almost anything to achieve victory. Competition to be the
"winner" has spawned an entire industry of SEO
consultants for hire. Organizations that have become
reasonably successful at optimization follow best practices
for on-page SEO, have great internal linking structure, and
run inbound linking campaigns. At the end of the day,
however, what often separates good rankings from great
rankings is the sheer amount of useful content that your
organization can generate on a regular basis.

Right now you're probably thinking, *"Here we go
again. Another lecture on the need for regularly updated
quality content."* Unfortunately, if you want to be
competitive, you're right. Today's B2B marketers are an

overtaxed bunch. They're often asked to do more now with fewer resources than they might have enjoyed a few years ago. But fortunately, if your organization is a products company, you probably already have a wealth of content that could be helping your current search rankings.

Most companies keep their knowledge bases, customer communities, and forums under lock and key, afraid that competitors or prospects may see their warts or proprietary information. The reality is that your documentation and community sites likely contain a tremendous amount of content that can and should be indexable by search engines. Assuming your documentation is complete and your community is well taken care of, you have nothing to hide. Competitors probably already know more about you than you can imagine, and prospects will likely be encouraged by the transparency and happy to have access to your community during the buying process.

Any time one of your support reps answers a question via email but does not have relevant documentation to link to, he or she should write up an answer, post it to the site, and send the URL to the client. Of course, it helps if you have a simple content management system, a community management system, or a user forum so that your reps can adopt this standardized process with zero IT involvement. This allows your support team and also your user community to become content creators for you. You'll find that the number of pages indexed on your documentation or community site quickly outstrips your corporate site and that you start to rank well for many long tail keywords. Who wouldn't want to double or triple their number of quality pages in Google or Bing's indexes?

What can you start making available to the search engines? Consider creating and promoting easily accessible content such as product documentation, FAQs, blogs, community forums, and idea exchanges. And who says that a support ticket can't be an opportunity for SEO-boosting content? Think outside the box to come out ahead in the great SEO race.

Chapter 7. Quantifying Success

A recent study by the Sales Lead Management Association (SLMA) polled 140 small to mid-sized businesses (<250 employees) and found some interesting results that confirm the ongoing problem of siloed sales and marketing efforts. The study found that nearly 63% of these companies are unable to calculate ROI for their marketing activities. The main reason cited was a lack of feedback on lead status from their sales teams. But marketers have to take some share of the blame. More than half (56%) of respondents said their marketing teams don't qualify their leads before passing them off to sales. This classic communication breakdown between sales and marketing is really at the heart of the problem.

The SLMA study also found that the predominant attitude marketers took toward this situation is that sales should qualify its own leads. Most respondents said their businesses have not found a reliable way to coordinate the efforts of their sales and marketing teams.[21]

The persistent disconnect between sales and marketing illustrated by this study can exist regardless of company size or industry vertical. Because they tend to operate under different philosophies and different incentive systems, sales and marketing teams often seem engaged in a perpetual tug-of-war, with each department feeling misunderstood, undervalued, and overwhelmed with petty obstacles and hassles. Marketers often feel that their company's sales team doesn't appreciate their creative lead generation efforts, not to mention all of the work that goes into designing the website, building the brand, and developing the corporate image. Similarly, the sales team is convinced that marketing people just don't get it: All leads are *not* created equal. To make matters worse, management always hints that salespeople could be a bit more industrious, while the marketing department—often viewed as a cost center rather than a revenue-driving engine—must continually struggle to justify its budget.

The adoption of a marketing automation solution can change these adversarial dynamics, putting everybody on the same team, all pulling together on the same rope for a better bottom line. In a September 2009 report entitled *B2B Lead Management Automation Market Overview*, Laura

Ramos of Forrester Research had this to say about the kind of change that marketing automation can effect:

> Bickering between sales and marketing over lead quality and sales' responsiveness to marketing-generated demand ends when firms implement LMA [lead management automation] technology. The routing, monitoring, and reporting features let marketers demonstrate the team's impact on sales pipelines and show how marketing activity makes the sales process more efficient.[22]

The Forrester report cites three case studies of firms whose marketing departments demonstrated quantifiable value by aligning marketing activity with sales results. One company quadrupled the number of webinars offered and subsequently increased participation by more than 30%. Another company with a small sales team employed marketing automation to increase sales efficiency and improved reps' opportunity-to-close rates by more than 15% as a result. Finally, a larger company implemented a solution that enabled its sales and marketing teams to work together effectively for the first time by using lead scoring and grading along with prospect tracking to qualify leads before guiding them into the sales pipeline.[23]

The ability to deliver more highly qualified leads, along with being able to track every online marketing effort, is a powerful equation for success for sales and marketing teams alike.

Campaign ROI Calculator

Until recently, applying the concept of accountability to marketing teams amounted to little more than glorified guesswork. Tracking in any traditional sense was nearly impossible, and the disconnect between marketing and sales processes prevented any kind of meaningful data analysis. This lack of accountability has long contributed to wasted marketing spend and missed opportunities. You can, and should, know every dollar you're spending and every dollar you're making from each individual marketing investment.

Luckily, this is becoming less and less of a problem for marketers. Marketing automation tools make it possible to track every online effort in which you invest. By tying your CRM's sales opportunity data to campaign results, a marketing automation platform helps you calculate and track the trajectory of ROI for every campaign you launch, giving you true visibility into pipeline and revenue.

Marketing automation solutions generally contain reporting tools for tracking every campaign on large and small scales. Collecting data, analyzing metrics, calculating ROI, and reporting the results is as easy as one, two, three.

Transform your marketing automation solution into that handy campaign ROI calculator you've always wanted by following these three easy steps:

1. **Tie costs to campaign.** Create an individual campaign for each of your marketing efforts. For example, a trip to a trade show may be tied to one particular campaign, while an email sponsorship would be applicable to another. Then enter the associated costs for each campaign in your marketing automation solution, and tag future prospects with the appropriate campaign.

2. **Tie campaigns to leads.** You can associate your leads with a certain campaign by tagging your targeted landing pages with that campaign. Each new visitor who converts will carry the associated campaign as the point of origin. Leads that are collected offline, such as at a trade show, can be tagged when they are imported into your database.

3. **Collect the right metrics.** Once your campaign data is entered and your leads are tagged, you can start tracking your metrics. To determine the effectiveness of your campaigns, consider a few different numbers:

   - Number of new leads per campaign
   - Number of qualified leads (usually those leads you pass on to sales) per campaign

- Number of opportunities per campaign, or the opportunity value of those leads

Since your prospects are tagged with the appropriate campaign, you can easily create reports that help you produce these metrics. Those reports will tell you not only where you've been, but more importantly, they'll give you direction on where you want to go in the future. Once you know which campaigns are performing the best, you can use that data to adjust your spend and maximize ROI. A good marketing automation solution should come with reporting capabilities that collect data to calculate such metrics and produce reports on them. You can also sync your marketing automation platform with your CRM for seamless opportunity tracking.

Integration of Paid Search

The integration of paid search (advertising via search engines) with a marketing automation platform adds another valuable benefit in that it provides easy ROI reporting of your paid search campaigns. AdWords campaigns are automatically and continuously updated and refreshed within the platform, and built-in reporting tools allow you to go well beyond the typical cost per click. Other measurement indices track data to compare costs and to calculate the true cost of a prospect. The reporting tool calculates:

- Number of clicks
- Cost per vetted prospect
- Cost per opportunity
- Cost per sale
- Cost per campaign
- Marketing ROI

Most marketing automation platforms also have the ability to sync with Google Analytics for more extensive data analysis. Once you have accurate data, you can calculate the ROI for different keyword niches, which in turn provides insight into many other areas, such as determining which customer segmentations to pursue and in what order to address them. The end result is the value— the proof in the pudding—of your marketing endeavors. Having an established system for tracking your spend and boosting your results will make justifying that marketing budget much easier next year.

AUTOMATION REVOLUTION

If there's any caveat to the seemingly limitless capabilities and benefits that marketing automation offers, it's that adopting a marketing automation solution and using it according to best practices will most likely require a dramatic, almost revolutionary, change in your company's business approach and philosophy. This is where it's crucial to be able to think outside of the inbox to expand your online marketing toolkit beyond email alone.

One company that we know of embraced this sort of revolutionary change and achieved excellent results. Demand Metric is a management advisory firm that produces executive summaries, how-to guides, practical templates and tools, and consulting solutions for sales and marketing executives in mid-sized enterprises. At the start of 2008, Demand Metric still had not ventured into online marketing and lead generation through the internet. Their sales model was based on cold calling, with each representative making between 100 and 200 calls each day. On average, the team made one sale for every 328 calls. But because the sales team had no way to gauge prospect interest or determine which leads were most sales-ready, they were not able to efficiently prioritize their efforts.

But soon after implementing a marketing automation solution, Demand Metric was able to start launching online campaigns and qualifying leads so that its sales team could better allocate their time. Using forms and enticing visitors with special offers, Demand Metric began converting visitors to leads from their website. Demand Metric received so many incoming leads that there were simply too many for the sales team to follow up with. As a solution, they began placing prospects on a drip marketing track that would allow them to keep in touch as well as gain additional opportunitics for interaction with prospects. Through integration with salesforce.com, the sales team was able to easily adopt a marketing automation solution as part of their process.

Within the first month of using their marketing automation solution, Demand Metric experienced a drastic change in theirs sales model and quickly realized the following tangible benefits:

- Prior to adopting a marketing automation solution, it took an average of 328 calls to make one sale. With the qualified leads generated by their marketing automation solution, conversion rates increased dramatically, averaging one sale for every 70 calls.

- In their previous model, about one in 12 product demos resulted in a sale. After implementing a marketing automation solution, that number rose to one in three. The sales team had to do less work to achieve the same or a higher level of sales due to vast improvements in the sales team's efficiency.[24]

"It's reasonable to expect a 300% increase in conversions within the first few months when implementing online lead generation with a marketing automation platform."

Jesse Hopps, CEO, Demand Metric

The Demand Metric experience illustrates several of the core messages communicated in this book. Recall the iconic Fuller Brush man with his non-competitive bounded sales territory and the ease with which he created one-to-one relationships with customers through cold calling. Those cold calling tactics worked. They still work. They were working for Demand Metric. But the process was highly labor-intensive, which made it both inefficient and costly. While the fundamentals of the sales cycle may essentially remain the same, and people, still being people, will always prefer to buy from other human beings who treat them as valued individuals, marketing and sales teams can no longer afford to ignore the new paradigms of the digital marketplace.

Demand Metric found a way to embrace those new realities, but it required a fairly radical change to a sales model that places far less emphasis on cold calling as the preferred path to lead generation. The Demand Metric experience is a great test, but it chronicles only some of the revolutionary changes that must happen in any business model that wants to make the most effective possible use of a marketing automation solution.

Even if your company doesn't rely heavily on cold calls, or if you're already well along in the development of your internet marketing strategies, your marketing team's approach might still emphasize quantity over quality in the area of lead generation. While having an abundance of leads is generally considered to be a good thing, marketing automation as a philosophy emphasizes the *quality* of those leads—that is, the only leads that truly matter are the really good ones. This new way of thinking can represent a significant paradigm shift for your company. But the benefits you'll reap by adopting a marketing automation solution far outweigh the minor challenge of making that transition.

Marketing automation goes a very long way in helping B2B companies confront many of the challenges presented by broader market opportunity and a longer, more complex, and increasingly depersonalized sales cycle. Marketing automation tools put a face on our prospects through scoring and grading, and web analytics features provide insight into prospect needs, behaviors, and interests. They also nudge us to treat prospects with dignity through adopting permission-based marketing practices and by aligning our message with their issues, objectives, and concerns.

Marketing automation also makes it easy for a company to demonstrate product knowledge and deliver thought leadership and highly personalized email messaging. It gives us a dialogue tool for connecting authentically with our customers, in turn offering them real value through targeted content with information on relevant topics.

Marketing automation helps build business relationships for the long haul by making it easy to stay in touch with both prospects and customers by checking in periodically and nurturing them even beyond the closed sale.

THE QUESTION OF COST

Marketing automation solutions are typically offered as a hosted solution via the SaaS model. Pricing currently ranges from $500 to $5,000 per month, and tiered pricing lets you pay only for those services you need. The standard subscription-based model is available from some vendors that don't require a contract. For small and mid-sized businesses looking for value in a tight economy, even these prices may seem prohibitive. But the costs of *not* adopting a marketing automation solution may be far greater.

Here are some points to consider when evaluating the costs and benefits of implementing a marketing automation solution:

- How much time and money could you save by consolidating your tools and automating your email campaigns?

- How much more effective could your marketing and sales teams be if their respective tools were synced in a coordinated platform with a unified interface?

- How much value could you gain by coordinating your marketing efforts with your sales cycle goals?

- How much could you enhance the efficiency of your marketing and sales teams by eliminating incorrect, incomplete, or redundant data?

- How many more opportunities could you create if you were able to nurture and follow up with each and every promising lead instead of letting some of them fall through the cracks?

- How much easier would it be to demonstrate your marketing team's influence on pipeline and revenue if you had analytics data and automatically generated reports to help you calculate ROI?

- How much more smoothly would your business run if sales and marketing teams cooperated effectively to achieve your company's desired goals?

This book is only a starting point. You'll have to answer these questions for yourself. But if there's one takeaway from this book, it's that marketing automation truly is the most transformative advancement in sales and marketing since the advent of the CRM. Now is the time for you to harness its power: Think outside the inbox.

Notes

Chapter 1. Marketing: What's New?

[1] SiriusDecisions, *Buying In to Longer Sales Cycles* research brief (Southport, CT: SiriusDecisions, 2009).

[2] Brian J. Carroll, *Lead Generation for the Complex Sales Cycle* (New York: McGraw-Hill, 2006).

[3] Forrester Research, *CRM Market Size and Forecast: 2006 to 2010* (Cambridge, MA: Forrester Research, 2006).

Chapter 2. A Clearing in the Cloud

[4] Karen Talavera, "Three Ways to Personalize Your Email Marketing: Remember Who You're Talking To," *Marketing Profs* (May 19, 2009) http://www.marketingprofs.com/9/remember-who-youre-talking-to-email-talavera.asp

Chapter 3. The Four T's of Effective Email Campaigns

[6] Mark Brownlow, Assessing the Best Time to Send Email, *Email Marketing Reports* (June 2, 2009) http://www.email-marketing-reports.com/iland/2009/06/assessing-best-time-to-send-email.html

Chapter 4. Looking for Love in All the Wrong Places

[7] Brian J. Carroll, "On Lead Generation: Insist on Lead Quality Over Quantity," *B2B Lead Generation Blog* (July 1, 2009) http://blog.startwithalead.com/weblog/2009/07/insist-on-quality-over-quantity-.html?no_prefetch=

[8] Mac McIntosh, "A List of B2B Lead Qualification Criteria by Category," *Sales Leads Insights* (August 1, 2009) http://www.sales-lead-insights.com/2009/a-list-of-b2b-lead-qualification-criteria-by-category/#high_4

[9] HubSpot, *Who's Blogging What* ebook (February 23, 2010) http://www.hubspot.com/whos-blogging-what/

[10] HubSpot, *State of Facebook for Business* report [PDF], p. 7 (December 28, 2009) http://www.hubspot.com/blog/bid/5427/HubSpot-Releases-State-of-Facebook-for-Business-Report-Offers-Live-Webinar

[11] Drew Neisser, "In Social Media, Point-of-View Equals ROI," *MultiChannel Merchant* (November 13, 2009) http://multichannelmerchant.com/social-media/1113-social-media-point-of-view/ Number of followers and followed Twitter accounts updated from JetBlue's Twitter page (April 27, 2010) http://twitter.com/JetBlue/

[12] Pardot, *Omnipress case study* (2009) http://www.pardot.com/clients/case-studies/case-study-omnipress.html

Chapter 5. Staying in Touch

[13] Dan McDade, "Why Sales Needs Even Fewer Leads, Even In Tight Times," *CRM Marketplace* (July 23, 2009) http://www.crmmarketplace.com/article.mvc/Why-Sales-Needs-Fewer-Leads-Even-In-Tight-Tim-0001

[14] "Velocity of Lead Follow-Up Is Critical To Winning the Complex Sale," *B2B Lead Generation Blog* (May 24, 2005) http://blog.startwithalead.com/weblog/2005/05/speed_of_sales_.html

[15] Smith-Harmon, *Retail Welcome Email Benchmark Study* (March 10, 2009) http://www.smith-harmon.com/resources/2009/03/retail_welcome_ email_benchmark_study.php

[16] Ardath Albee, "Help B2B Buyers Find Their Place in the Story," *Marketing Interaction Blog* (March 29, 2010) http://marketinginteractions.typepad.com/marketing_interactions/2010/03/help-b2b-buyers-find-their-place-in-the-story.html

[17] Lori Feldman, "Nine Must-Have Drip Marketing Campaigns," *The ACT! by Sage Journal* (November 4, 2009) http://community.act.com/t5/The-ACT-by-Sage-Journal/Nine-Must-Have-Drip-Marketing-Campaigns-Guest-Blog-by-Lori/ba-p/57345

[18] Quoted in Lori Feldman, ibid.

Chapter 6. Making the Most of What You've Got

[19] MarketingSherpa, "Product Demo with Voluntary Registration Results in 23% Conversion Rate" [INTTRA case study] (February 18, 2009) https://www.marketingsherpa.com/barrier.html?ident=31050

[20] Ardath Albee, "Lift Revenues 70% By Cleaning Up Dirty B2B Data," *Marketing Interaction Blog* (January 2, 2009) http://marketinginteractions.typepad.com/marketing_interactions/2009/01/lift-revenues-70-by-cleaning-up-dirty-b2b-data.html

Chapter 7. Quantifying Success

[21] The Velos Group, SLMA's *2009 Lead Management Practice Survey Results* (February 11, 2010) http://www.salesleadmgmtassn.com/ news/2009-velos-study-results-b2b-roi.htm

[22] Laura Ramos, *B2B Lead Management Automation Market Overview*, Forrester Research (September 22, 2009) http://www.forrester.com/rb/Research/b2b_lead_management_automation_market_overview/q/id/47318/t/2

[23] Ibid.

[24] Pardot, *Demand Metric Case Study* (2008) http://www.pardot.com/ clients/case-studies/case-study-demand-metric.html